Advance praise for ThinkAbout

"The verb I would use for *ThinkAbout* is **DARE,** as Andrea encourages, cajoles, convinces and assures us that we can create what works and what's right for our brand."

Mim Harrison, Brand Strategist, Levenger

"Andrea Syverson's new book, *ThinkAbout,* challenges you to ask the hard questions and forces you to stop and think. You can sail through many because you already focused on those topics, they lie in your comfort zone. **I dare you to take the time on the hard ones and really stop and think, and work through the questions and see how much better your products are in the end."**

Sheryl Clark, President, Boston Proper

"From the storyselling genius of Girl Scout Thin Mints to the respect for men's shaving elevated by Harry's, **Andrea's insightful prompts and provocative vignettes will have you thinking differently about your merchandising and product development efforts."**

Laura Brady, President, Medical Positioning

"Andrea IS a verb! And her action is 'getting it.' She gets it because she is purposeful in her approach. Through the innovative, verb-saturated examples and exercises in *ThinkAbout,* she'll help lead you and your brand team to create even more inspired products that your customers can't wait to get!"

Rosemary Harris, originator, writer, designer, Really Woolly® Cards.

"Dive *anywhere* into this book—**you'll discover a new lens to view your own team.** Give it a little reflection, maybe provoke a few discussions . . . and invent your own unique process to keep things fresh *whatever* your product or service. **The bonus: you will be reminded that our work can be—ought to be—joyful, life-giving, and creative!"**

Ted Ehrlichman, COO, Suncoast Workforce

"Inspiring brand stories abound in *ThinkAbout,* and Andrea's engaging writing makes delving into each an absolute pleasure. **Andrea's thought-provoking prompts help you turn inspiration into action, finding creative new ways to push your brand and your products further than ever.** I highly recommend this book to anyone looking to be better than 'good.'"

Paal Gisholt, President & CEO, SmartPak

"Andrea breaks down the complex and complicated into manageable, small steps anyone can take who wants to make their brand resonate with customers. **She makes brands come alive with a focus on action words—what special and unique values do brands deliver to their customers and how can you learn to transform your brand by breaking it down into its component value deliverables** . . . with Andrea's commitment to analyzing what unique values these exemplary brands deliver through action, **her book is committed to helping you translate new understanding into action for your brand."**

Pam Danziger, Unity Marketing

"Thought provoking! A jump-start that will expand the critical thinking process in development meetings. *ThinkAbout* ignites energy and rigor to a process that ensures customer delight!"

Michele Fortune, President, DRG Network

"*ThinkAbout* is a conversation starter. Her use of verbs as creative prompts will help stimulate us to think, create and enhance the Fairytale Brownies brand."

Eileen Spitalny, Co-Founder, Fairytale Brownies

"Who doesn't love a good story, and Andrea is a natural storyteller. In *ThinkAbout*, she invites the reader to shift her gaze and try on a different way of thinking and branding. **Her words are wise, approachable and plenty of fun.**"

Ellen Kresky, Creative Director, Ben & Jerry's

"What is a brand, really? It is an emotional connection. So in developing a brand, and then living true to it, we marketers, merchants, and business owners, have to ask ourselves: What is it that we want our customers to feel? It all starts there. And, feeling is intricately tied with action— with verbs. **That's what makes Andrea's *ThinkAbout* approach so wonderful. She prompts brand builders by asking what is your unique VERB. Find that and from there your brand will unfold!**"

Terri S. Alpert, CEO, Uno Alla Volta

"**A must-read for every marketer and brand-builder! Andrea Syverson brings her trademark passion and fire to the brand development process** in a thought-provoking, easy-to-digest format that gives the reader concrete tips and real-world advice for building better brands. This book will go front and center in my office bookshelf!"

Patty Dowd Schmitz, COO, Chicago Concours Inc.

"In *ThinkAbout*, Andrea Syverson continues her magical storytelling about products and brands. **I marvel how she gets me to read a page and then gaze out the window to ponder what I hadn't pondered before. Her stories are not only truly useful for product developers, they are just plain fun.**"

Steve Leveen, President & Co-Founder, Levenger

"I am eager to put a copy of *ThinkAbout* in the hands of every one of our product development and innovation leaders, **and even more eager to watch Andrea's work tease forth our next generation of great products.**"

John M. Vitek, President & CEO, Saint Mary's Press

"*ThinkAbout* is a merchant's playbook. Inspiring, motivating, and most importantly, Andrea gets the reader to 'think' about merchandise in a new way. **Think of it as a blueprint for creative product development.**"

Tim Littleton, President & CEO, CHEFS

"**Andrea's approach, passion and methodologies immediately guide a company to the right path.** Andrea and I have worked with mutual clients from gifts, food, and apparel—the outcome is always the same: Andrea's talent and depth of knowledge helps the client think differently, act differently and more importantly, the company is changing to meet the needs of its customers."

Gina Valentino, President, Hemisphere Marketing

ThinkAbout

77 Creative Prompts
for Innovators

ANDREA SYVERSON

PMP

Paramount Market Publishing, Inc.

Paramount Market Publishing, Inc.
950 Danby Road, Suite 136
Ithaca, NY 14850
www.paramountbooks.com
Voice: 607-275-8100; 888-787-8100   Fax: 607-275-8101

Publisher: James Madden
Editorial Director: Doris Walsh

This publication is designed to provide accurate and authoritative information in regard to the subject matter covered for educational purposes only. It is sold with the understanding that the publisher is not engaged in rendering legal, accounting, or other professional services. If legal advice or other expert assistance is required, the services of a competent professional should be sought.

Cataloging in Publication Data available

ISBN-10: 0-9851795-3-8 | ISBN-13: 978-0-9851795-3-3

For all my clients, who have graciously allowed me
to put verbs into action as I partnered with them
in the joyful work of strengthening their brands
and product lines. It has been an honor.

And for Dean. Thank you for masterfully living one verb
on a daily basis, both in and out of the office: *love*.

Table of Verbs

Go ahead and flip this book open to a verb that tickles your imagination — you can start from the middle and read forward or backward or sideways or absolutely any which way—it just doesn't matter! *ThinkAbout* is meant to be a muse for your imagination. The verbs drove the product selections. Many products share other verb tendencies and many other stories could be told for each verb. It's a playful and bite-sized approach to fit into your busy work life. Use it as a creative springboard!

Introduction

I had the honor of going on an enlightening branding walkabout in Australia for one of my global clients. It was my second extensive trip to this country. I like the Aussies—their independent spirit, their love of adventure, their casualness, and their humbleness. In the midst of this deep cultural immersion, I visited 8 cities in 8 weeks all across the country and met with over 60 of the client's stakeholders. In these facetime tête-à-têtes, we talked frankly and openly about the challenges facing this company's existing product line, its present pricing structure, its future competitive arena, and how it would need to adapt to the particulars of this niche Australian marketplace to be more customer-centric. I believe deeply in this kind of research. In first-hand observation, in being *with* your stakeholders in their environments, in deep listening, in thinking deliberately about all the brand variables, in following curiosities, in questioning.

After posing a question to one of these important stakeholders, she paused thoughtfully before replying and said, "I'd like to give that a thinkabout." I smiled. Not only did I love hearing the Aussies' expressions, I liked that she took my question seriously and wanted to answer reflectively versus impulsively. I told her that "thinkabout" was a concept I wanted to take back to the States. Wouldn't we all benefit from building more thinkabout time into our busy work lives?

Randy Komisar, general partner at Kleiner Perkins Caufield & Byers, wrote, "What we need is a set of constant provocations." My time in Australia was just that—a set of constant provocations. It was fascinating to see life through a different lens from the simple things like grocery shopping and banking and popular culture to how schools and churches and eateries are simultaneously similar and different from our stateside equivalents. My head spun with intriguing product names, promotional concepts, and simply amusing phrases like describing two opposites as "chalk and cheese" or someone a bit conceited as suffering from "tall poppy syndrome." It proved fruitful on many levels.

I have been a long time student of Harvard Business School professor Clayton Christensen. My Australian sojourn validated the importance of the five verbs and descriptions he outlines in *The Innovator's DNA: Mastering the Five Skills of Disruptive Innovators*—the book he co-authored with Jeff Dyer and Hal Gregersen (Harvard Business Review Press, 2011)—as crucial for developing new ideas, products and services:

- **Associating**—drawing connections between questions, problems, or ideas from unrelated fields

- **Questioning**—posing queries that challenge common wisdom

- **Observing**—scrutinizing the behavior of customers, suppliers, and competitors to identify new ways of doing things

- **Networking**—meeting people with different ideas and perspectives

- **Experimenting**—constructing interactive experiences and provoking unorthodox responses to see what insights emerge

I, too, am partial to verbs. My Aussie honeymoon walkabout inspired my first book: *BrandAbout™ A Seriously Playful Approach for Passionate Brand-Builders and Merchants.* It centers around 10 verbs: play, be, listen, conduct, dare, herald, craft, practice, kindle, and integrate—all of which I actively engage in with my clients when I am listening, strategizing, visioning, advising, and prompting! Creative branding and merchandising innovation are so linked together that my work as a provocateur often overlaps both disciplines. In product development and merchandising creation, I let another one of Christensen's profound axioms guide my work: "A product has a job to do for your customer." I extend his concept and remind my clients that their products (or services) either enhance their brand or detract from it.

This book is all about products that enhance their brands and take Christensen's advice to heart. Positive product role models. Products and services that go to work for their brands each and every day advancing and delighting and enchanting and stretching and validating and welcoming. It has been a fun and fruitful journey of discovering product developers and service providers who go the extra mile to both woo and wow their customers. It is also a reminder of the serious rigor it takes to turn brands into Lovemarks.

You may remember that it was Saatchi & Saatchi's CEO Kevin Roberts who coined this term, Lovemarks. It is simply defined this way: "Lovemarks are brands that reach your heart as well as your mind, creating an intimate, emotional connection that you just can't live without. Ever."

Products that have captured my attention are actively doing a job for their customers and enhancing their brands. They are products that have come across my radar because I have worked with their creators as clients or I have had some firsthand personal experience with them or they have simply provoked my curiosity and admiration. I have included 77 product examples from a wide assortment of industries (fashion, gourmet food, travel, nonprofits). Products that speak to different target audiences (outdoor enthusiasts, children, gardeners, luxury). Products that are in some cases actually services or programs. Products and verbs that I hope will provide inspiration for those whose daily jobs it is to create the next Lovemarks.

Creating products that woo and wow customers day after day is tough and demanding work. I know. I've been in the trenches doing it for two decades. It is easy and tempting to take shortcuts. To crank out the next new thing to fill a slot, a shelf, a collection, to meet a madcap deadline. Aisles and stores and sites and landfills are filled with this kind of clutter, with products that don't fit Roberts' or Christensen's or my criteria. This is not a book about those.

But product development is also joyful work. Life-giving, creative work. And, absolutely heartwarming to receive exuberant reactions from customers who are gratified that you took the time to thinkabout how this product would solve one of their pain points or how it could evoke emotions or how it simply fascinates and owning it becomes part of a person's mélange of "can't live withouts." This book is about those products. There are many, many other products like these that I could have included (the book continues in a blog! See ierpartners.com). As a matter of fact, entire books have been written about some of these examples. I purposefully did not choose those. I actually started with the verbs. In many cases I spoke with the leaders of these companies directly and we had great verby chats. For others, I conducted primary and secondary research as both a customer and a merchandising professional. Each of these product vignettes have larger chapters and stories behind their narratives. My purpose in this book was to give you just a stanza or two of information to spark your innovative thinking.

In hindsight, adjectives would have been easier. All sorts of products are charming, brighter, bolder, newer and promise they'll change your life! Superlative adjectives abound. I wanted an action-oriented and more holistic approach to product development connected to brand promises. I wanted to showcase how products are meant to support brand missions. It had to be verbs.

Like *BrandAbout, ThinkAbout* is meant to be a seriously playful, action-oriented process in and of itself. A creative prompt. A bit of inspiration. A morsel of merchandising muse that can be flipped open when the creative juices run dry. Read what one brand did with a particular verb. Give that a thinkabout for your brand: is it relevant? Does it ignite new thinking? Lead to a curiosity that needs exploring? Invite a new perspective? If not, flip to another and try that one on for size. Play with one or two or all 77 verbs for your product line. Or, pick your favorite letter! Or, start your own list. There are no rules. It's meant to be a fun dashboard of ideas to help you get your next one!

In addition to showcasing each product example and how the verb plays out for that particular brand, I have asked a few questions to jumpstart the creative conversation process. Think of these as a gentle tap on the shoulder, an outside nudge, a bit of a constant provocation. That's always what I've seemed to need to do my best work.

So, go ahead, take time for a *ThinkAbout.* It's good for your product-creating soul!

hen is the last time you received a handwritten note from a fellow business colleague? A short but precise note expressing appreciation for a job well done? Conversely, when was the last time *you* took the time to write one yourself? In today's "always on" culture, we are more likely to text our praise or dash off a quick email. IF we remember. IF we take the five minutes. IF we have the right tools on hand.

Brad Darooge, President & CEO of Baudville, a business supplier of recognition materials, celebrates those online efforts but wants to make it even easier to orchestrate moments like that more often— and with good old fashioned paper. Baudville believes that putting applause on paper matters and they've built a brand as the go-to place for daily recognition. "You wouldn't believe how much a handwritten note really makes a difference. I see how people post our notes in their cubicles, or take them home to show their families or keep them in a file folder tucked inside their desks. Praise matters. The tangibility factor matters too. Really, how many people print out an email? A handwritten notecard that can be kept, displayed or reread really matters. We need more of this positive mojo in the workplace!"

So, of course, the brilliant product developers at Baudville came up with just the right thing to encourage more interoffice applauding: The YOU ROCK! Cheers Kit, a complete toolbox of exclamatory notes and formats that leave just the right space for a personal handwritten message. "We make it easy and fun," Darooge says. "We know how busy managers are and how hard perhaps it might be to come up with the right words."

Darooge believes applause needs to be a cultural value, no matter what size your organization. "All types of personal praises are very meaningful.

Praise isn't just a top down task. Many times, it's even more meaningful when it's done laterally, peer-to-peer. Our Shout Outs are a clever tool to celebrate your co-workers "good behavior" loud and clear! We've created a fresh, contemporary way to enable more applause in the workplace. We want giving recognition in the office to be as common and natural as getting that cup of coffee each day."

applaud

ThinkAbout: APPLAUD

What is it about your product that makes people want to clap?
How might your product prompt your customers to do something they know they need to do but need a bit of a reminder?
Who on your product development team deserves a shout out?
How will you meaningfully applaud their efforts?

*i*n speaking with Deborah Delmage, Vice President, Merchandising & Brand of Gardener's Supply Company, it is obvious I am speaking to someone who loves what she does. She tells me she is not alone as Gardener's Supply is a company of gardeners. The company was first founded to encourage everyone to garden, including those with physical challenges. Since 1983 Gardener's Supply has had the same mission: "To spread the joys and rewards of gardening, because gardening nourishes the body, elevates the spirit, builds community and makes the world a better place."

Specializing in functional gardening products that assist in the challenges of this activity, Gardener's Supply offers a plethora of helps to cultivate its customers' lifetime love of gardening—no matter if they are beginners or award-winning gardeners. One of these "helps" is its exclusive Elevated Cedar Raised Bed, a product that Delmage and her team developed at their Vermont factory. Not only is it made in America, this product is both so beautiful and functional you almost want to bring it *inside* your house!

Delmage shares: "Our mission is to help customers be successful in their gardening endeavors. We designed the Elevated Raised Bed to help them garden without bending. It not only allows them to cultivate their passion more easily and happily, but we've had feedback that it solves other issues as well. Here's how we describe it:

> Bring your garden up to a whole new level! Our 2' x 8' elevated bed is easy to plant, tend and harvest without kneeling or bending. Plus, it offers creative landscaping opportunities. Set up one or more of these rectangular beds around the edge of your patio to add privacy, or arrange several along a perimeter to create a garden "room." Like our other cedar raised beds, the sides are held in place with our sleek and sturdy aluminum corners. There's a false floor made from marine-grade plywood set 10" down from the top so there's plenty of root space for vegetables and flowers. Floor has holes for drainage; vents in the sides allow air to circulate and excess moisture to evaporate.

A customer summarized his experience with this product in just two words: "LOVE 'EM!" He goes on to say, "My wife and I both are very

cultivate

pleased with these planters. They solved low back problems while making it enjoyable to plant the high maintenance crops like beans, peas, lettuce, greens and others that you want to stagger yields through the full garden season. They were extremely easy to assemble. Well worth the cost, for they should last decades with easy maintenance."

I count at least five reasons in his testimonial why this Elevated Cedar Raised Bed is a must have. In addition, it reinforces Gardener's Supply heritage! This company tends to its product functionality in a very purposeful way. Its customers count on them for this.

ThinkAbout: CULTIVATE

How do your products assist in cultivating your customers' vocations? Do your products accommodate a range of your customers' capabilities? How can your products be more multi-functional?

$\mathcal{W}$here does the verb *respect* fit in your brand's DNA? For Jeffrey Raider and Andy Katz-Mayfield, the two co-founders of Harry's, an online men's shaving boutique, this verb dominates their strategy. Here's how the two describe their service:

> Like most of you, we've long had to choose between over-priced, over-marketed razors that disrespect your intelligence, and low quality, cheap razors that disrespect your face. We knew there had to be a better way, so we created Harry's as a return to the essential: a great shave at a fair price.

Respecting customer intelligence, respecting the customer's face, lathering in an edited and simplified shopping experience (like one of these men did in his first business—Warby Parker) and creating a meaningful charitable connection all adds up to a new venture that elevates a daily chore. Harry's believes "a great shave is powerful, preparing you to conquer the world in your own way, every day."

It is apparent that this respect for their customer's time, attention and wallet coupled with respect for the activity of shaving informed all Raider's and Katz-Mayfield's brand launch decisions. The co-founders conducted their own shave tests and found all existing products on the market lacking. In addition to finding a European manufacturer to make a different type of blade, it led them to reconfigure the razor handles and craft two unique and exclusive Harry offerings: The Winston and The Truman, inspired by old pens and knives.

"With Harry's," Raider says in a *Fast Company* interview, "I think we care about customers a lot, but it's more about respecting them and giving them a product they really like, but not overwhelming them with choice—just sort of giving them a shaving tool we think will work really well."

Respect is also carried forward towards non-customers: "We can't imagine a more deserving group of skilled leaders than our veterans and The Mission Continues Fellows and are proud to give a shave to The Mission Continues." Harry's shares more about this organization on its website:

> The Mission Continues empowers veterans of recent wars to apply the skills they learned in the military here at home through six-month fellowships

with a non-profit organization. Through the fellowship program, they renew their own sense of purpose and better the lives of those around them.

In her very own memorable way, Aretha Franklin reminds us that everyone is just "asking for a little respect." The cofounders at Harry's remind us too.

ThinkAbout: RESPECT

As a product creator and merchant, what are ways you show respect for your customers' time, attention, and wallet through your product development decisions? How do your competitors' show this same respect? What might you consider doing to set yourself apart and show "a little more respect"?

Sometimes you want to dash into a store (or website), hunt down your purchase, and leave promptly. Other times, a store, a site, an atmosphere is so compelling that you want to linger, and linger, and linger some more. Terrain is one of *those* kinds of places. It's part of the Urban Outfitters' family of creative retailers whose stated goal is "to offer a product assortment and an environment so compelling and distinctive that the customer feels an empathetic connection to the brand and is persuaded to buy."

Terrain was designed purposefully for leisurely strolls through all their "mini-terrains"—eclectic little rooms and areas that beckon customers with all sorts of indoor-outdoor lifestyle products they hope you'll find irresistible. The merchants have waved their magic fairy dust over everything: meals, merchandise assortments, and even web copy to create a menagerie you want to somehow recreate in your own life.

Terrain has elevated lingering to an art form with experiential pauses built into its brand DNA. Both stores have delicious "farm-to-table" restaurants that encourage spontaneous long lunches and Sunday brunches as well as scheduled events and workshops. Here's the invitation the Terrain restaurant in Glen Mills, Pennsylvania, puts forth:

> Share our local, organic meals with close family and friends as you create lasting memories in our charming antique greenhouse. Taking your personal style, interpreting it by our talented culinary team, and presenting it all in our horticultural setting, we'll create a truly unique experience for you and your guests. We work tirelessly to craft an environment that aesthetically and gastronomically reflects the cycle of the seasons.

President Wendy McDevitt shared this in a *Bloomberg* interview: "Customers typically spend 1.5 hours browsing Terrain and that can double to three hours if they're visiting the café and shopping between glasses of wine or lunch. The one thing you can't get in the cyberworld is the tactile experience and that won't go away."

Lingering happens online as well as you stroll through their three main categories with simple teasers like Garden + Outdoor, House + Home, Jewelry + Accessories. Spend time on Terrain's site and you'll want to know more about Branches + Bunches or what's in The Reading Room

linger

or what Wanderlust is all about. You are enticed by the plus and you aren't disappointed. The Bulletin, their eclectic, informative blog is like a gardening class, cooking class, landscaping class, and artist date all rolled into one lovely scroll you can't help but linger on . . .

ThinkAbout: LINGER

Just how irresistible are your products? Does your overall product experience invite lingering? Is it a sensory, tactile experience? What unusual product assortment combinations might you create to entice your customers to linger longer within your brand?

*C*an you recall what significant legislation was passed in 1972? It was Title IX—a law that required equal opportunities for men and women in federally funded sports and education programs. Quite the benefit for young girls at that time. I was one of them and without this happening, I wouldn't have been able to run track for our State Championship.

For Missy Park, founder of Title Nine, a multichanneler of stylish performance apparel for women, this legislation was so life-changing, allowing her to jump start a sports career that led to being on Yale's lacrosse, basketball, and tennis teams—that she named her company after it. She never forgot its benefits.

Title Nine is a fun, personal business that does not take itself too seriously, but does take its customers' needs very seriously. Always on the lookout for ways to improve its customers' sports apparel experiences, it doesn't let the word "impossible" stand in its way.

Here are two product examples that showcase how the brilliant merchants at Title Nine make it a full time job to find ways to continually benefit its female athletes:

Impossible Swim

"We were told it was impossible to design a swim top with the custom fit and support of a halter and without the pain that comes from cranking down the neck tie. Well our swim merchant has never met Impossible. So she worked closely with a surf-betty designer we know to develop a nifty system that ties in the back and anchors the chest band and shoulder straps in the center of our back. Voila! Support we can count on without that pain in the neck."

benefit

title nine

Dresses, Skirts & Skorts

CUSTOMER RATING

SIZE

2	4	6	8
10	12	14	XS
S	M	L	XL

COLOR

PRICING

☐ $30.00-$59.99 (9)
☐ $60.00-$99.99 (10)

INTRODUCING: SKIRTS SWB with benefits

Beneath the girly exterior of each of these skirts lies a hidden boy short that sets us free. Free from unintended exposure. Free to run, dance, swing, live. No one will ever know... you're wearing a skort.

| Dirt-In-The-Skirt SWB $69.00 | Solid Dream SWB $57.00 | The Right Stuff SWB $55.00 | Swing SWB $64.00 |
| Print Dream SWB $62.00 | Run Around SWB $59.00 | Stand-Out SWB $65.00 | Scamper SWB $49.00 |

Skirts with Benefits (SWB)

"Beneath the girly exterior of each of these skirts lies a hidden boy short that sets us free. Free from unintended exposure. Free to run, dance swing live. No one will ever know . . . you're wearing a skort."

ThinkAbout: BENEFIT

What are your product's benefits (fringe or otherwise)? Have you somehow gone the extra mile to bring your customers more benefits than your competitors? Are you showing them that you truly understand what benefits them most?

*b*y now we all are convicted about the powerful importance of storytelling and selling within our brands. We realize that narration is a two way street: we as merchants and product developers have a story to tell about our creations, but so do our customers. It is the intersection of both of these stories that truly provides the emotional energy of engagement that elevates products as brand ambassadors.

Pendleton is a brand that takes narration seriously. Their more than 150-year heritage started with this story:

> "The first Indian Trade Blanket rolls off the looms at our mill in Pendleton, Oregon. A year later, the first retail store opens in Seaside, Oregon. The Bishop family helps organize the first Pendleton Round-Up and in 1916 Roy Bishop congratulates Native American rodeo champion Jackson Sundown."

From this humble beginning, their iconic product stories unfolded—blankets, shirts and more. Pendleton has never stopped creating products that are "storyworthy." They dedicate significant space on their website to narrating their heritage. They want customers to know they are the real deal.

In conversation with Dean White, Pendleton's Chief Sourcing Officer, he shared the behind-the-scenes story about their Board Shirts, made famous by the Beach Boys. Yes, *those* Beach Boys! "The Beach Boys first called themselves the Pendletones and their "uniform" was our Pendleton shirts worn over tee shirts . . . really like a surfer's jacket. When they started to sing more about the California surf scene, they changed their name but not their clothes. The band wore our blue and charcoal plaid shirts on the covers of their albums in the 60s. Then, in 2002, we brought back the Board Shirt in the same plaid, re-named The Blue Beach Boys Plaid. It's still going strong . . . we have a strong surfer following but also with longshoremen and outdoorsmen of all types." That's Pendleton's side of the story.

Here's what some of their customers have to say about this Pendleton product staple today:

> "I bought my first one in 1957, as a freshman forestry student. Since then I've worn out probably six Board Shirts, during my long career as a ranger and professional skier. All your woolens are classics, ideally suited to the Pacific North West."

narrate

PENDLETON

MEN
Woven Shirts
Knit Shirts
Sweaters
Pants / Shorts
Blazers / Jackets
Outerwear
Ranch Style
Loungewear
Accessories
Shoes

REVIVAL OF
THE FITTEST

It's back. The washable
Umatilla Wool Board
Shirt with short sleeves
and a t

Any way you wear it,
our best-selling Board
Shirt is a winner.
Since '60s surfers
discovered it, guys
have made this
rugged shirt jac their
own for camping,
fishing, hanging out -
and all kinds of
boarding! And the
warm, naturally water-
resistant Umatilla wool
fabric is still woven in
our American mills.
Board Shirt:

Fitted Short Sleeve >
Regular Long Sleeve >

"Must be a nut—own over 30 Board Shirts, been wearing them for over 40 years. Best shirt to own—will always wear my Pendleton to all functions."

"I 'borrowed' my dad's Pendletons when I was in high school (graduated in '62!) until I outgrew his and had to buy my own. I've never lost the nostalgia, or appreciation for the Board Shirts, and they never go out of style."

Look at how heritage is woven into each story these customers narrate. These Board Shirts are chapters in their lives in addition to being key products in Pendleton's assortment. Pendleton knows the value of this two-way discourse. Like their fine wool, narrating is a verb woven into the very fabric of their brand.

ThinkAbout: NARRATE

What products are "storyworthy" in your assortment?
What's your customers' side of those stories? How have you leveraged that narration in building your brand?

*i*t is no small task to take on rewriting The Bible. Or, to take on making it more accessible for today's busy, multi-tasking, attention deficit readers. Pastor, professor, author and translator, Eugene Peterson, did just that in his retirement. However, it did begin while Peterson was the founding pastor at Christ the King Presbyterian Church in Baltimore, where he shepherded a small congregation for 29 years. He discovered that he was constantly paraphrasing the Bible stories he read each Sunday into contemporary language. He was trying to help his congregation see the wonder in those pages. He became a modern day translator, working from the original Greek and Hebrew texts.

Like those who have followed Apple's every move with its high tech product rollouts and versions, I have followed Peterson's Bible. I was first introduced to it when I was sourcing and developing products for a Christian catalog I helped launched many years ago. Peterson's work came out in mini-installments. First, it was just The New Testament, Psalms and Proverbs. Three million copies were sold. Then The Old Testament and Wisdom Books were released. Six million were sold. Then the History Books. Then finally the Full Edition Bible was released, seven full years from the first. This then began all sorts of new releases in new configurations from NavPress, the publisher of The Message.

(I often use the ad that NavPress ran in a trade publication to underscore the importance of continual product improvement. These product developers listened closely to their readers after each edition was published and never rested until all that customer feedback was curated into an even better product. A good lesson for all of us—never be satisfied, even with an award-winning bestseller!)

There were Messages with numbered verses, leather bound copies, a daily reading version, a student version, a children's version, a compact version, and even a version covered in pink for breast cancer awareness. My personal favorite is one called Conversations, in which Peterson's sermons, wise commentary, and excerpts from his other 30 books are interspersed appropriately throughout. It makes you feel as if you are

translate

With Almost 10 Million *Message* Readers, You'd Think We Would Be Satisfied.

having a conversation with him as you read the Holy Word. As of this writing, more than 16 million copies have been sold around the world. As NavPress states on its website, Peterson's translation has "become one of the most loved Bibles of our day."

I have had the honor of meeting Peterson. He is a humble man. His purpose in translating was simple: "The Message is a reading Bible. It is not intended to replace the excellent study Bibles that are available. My intent here (as it was earlier in my congregation and community) is simply to get people reading it who don't know that the Bible is readable at all, at least by them, and to get people who long ago lost interest in the Bible to read it again."

ThinkAbout: TRANSLATE

How have you translated your customers' unspoken needs into product benefits? Does your product translate into a beloved part of your customers' lives? What system do you have in place to translate your customer feedback into an even better product?

*W*hen a company's tagline is "The Art of Delight," it is hard to pick just one product that supports this theme. Garnet Hill, a multichanneler known for its original designs, unique mix of products, and refreshing point of view, brings me joy every time I see its catalog in my mailbox. It has earned a Masters in Smile and Delight.

Take its Hats and Mittens Advent calendar for example. This is no ordinary countdown calendar that kids yawn through waiting for the big day. No, the genius merchants at Garnet Hill innovated a traditional holiday concept in a way that makes it thoroughly their own. Who else would have thought of a handcrafted, pure wool Advent calendar made of mini hats and mittens? Who else would have created an adorable container that allows for mini-notes, little candies, or teensy presents for young or old alike?

Delight is weaved into all these customer responses:

"I bought this advent calendar several years ago and it has become a tradition. My eight year old son still gets excited when he sees me hanging this along our staircase banister every December 1st. Friends and family always comment on how cute it is and several have bought one of their own. If you don't have kids you could fill it with little notes to your hubby!!"

"This very long and wonderful Advent decoration is the best decoration! We hang it on our fireplace mantel and even my older children look forward to the surprises. This is one of the many Garnet Hill items that exceeded my expectations!"

"We have had soooo much fun with this gorgeous product. The knit details are beautiful and the family has had a lot of fun celebrating each day that leads closer to Christmas. The quality is better than expected. Get one before they are gone."

Garnet Hill brand leaders know that when delighting their customers is their full time job, the job of each product is to over deliver. And over delight!

delight

ThinkAbout: DELIGHT

Do your products make your customers smile? Consistently?
How can you add more delight to your product mix? To your
presentation? What refresh might you need to turn an
ordinary product concept into an extraordinary one?

*d*id anyone at your Thanksgiving table say this when they were passing the gravy: "I have always wanted a gravy boat with a top on it to keep the gravy warm. This one pours hot gravy out and keeps it warm throughout the whole meal. I love that the lid has a snug fit and rubber gasket to help seal in the heat. I ran it through the dishwasher in the top rack and it came out perfectly! PS Will try this for hot maple syrup for my next pancake breakfast! Love that I can heat syrup in the microwave and have it kept warm!"

Or, this when they were passing the meat platter around: "This divided platter makes presentation so much neater and prettier. I used the dividing ridge along the middle to hold bunches of grapes for garnish and that worked really well." Or, "My mother-in-law always serves two different kinds of meat at every holiday/family get together. I'm buying her one for Christmas and I want one too!"

These were just a few comments that Tim Littleton, President of CHEFS has heard from his customers about two recent innovative

new products: the Extra-Large Porcelain Gravy Boat and the Divided Serving Platter. Both of these now "holiday must-haves" are exclusive to CHEFS and were inspired by Littleton's own Thanksgiving dinner experience. "My wife and I had 20 people around our table last year. Like many families, we don't carve our turkey at the table. It's just too messy. I carved our bird in the kitchen and brought out the platter with an organized pile of white meat and dark meat so people didn't have to politely search and find the type of meat they really wanted. That's when I got the idea for the divided platter. And then I saw how we had to keep running back in the kitchen to warm up more gravy and refresh the small gravy boat. I thought if this is what's happening at our table, it's happening across all Thanksgiving gatherings. I knew CHEFS could solve this and we did!"

anticipate

Littleton is one of CHEFS' chief anticipators. He leads the company and product development team to constantly be on the hunt for ways to make their customers' lives easier and more productive in the kitchen. It's a full-time job but one that has helped set this niche player apart from other cooking companies. "Our merchants cook. They entertain family and friends. They know what products really work. We say 'The Best Kitchen Starts Here' because we try to stay one step (or more!) ahead of our customers. This is why our customers love us."

ThinkAbout: ANTICIPATE

What's your recipe for anticipating your customers' needs?
Have you rolled up your sleeves and kitchen-tested your
products and your competitors' to see what really works?
How are you articulating the solutions you've found?

"*M*aking incremental improvements is always a safer bet, but to really build a superior experience, sometimes you have to attack the *whole* problem with a systematic solution," says Paal Gisholt, CEO of SmartPak Equine. "What we did for equine health is kind of like what Apple did for the sale of digital music. Apple didn't just make a better MP3 player, they surrounded their iPod with iTunes, music content partnerships, and allowing the iTunes Store to sell individual songs. Systematic thinking allowed Apple to create an experience that solved the many problems that were holding back online sale of music.

"At SmartPak, we were trying to solve a problem in the billion dollar equine health industry—getting equine supplements and drugs to be fed right. It's quite a challenge, with barns of 30 or more horses all being fed different regimens and different dosages and staff that may not know much about horses and may not even speak English! We realized that to really solve all the problems—missed feedings, dose errors, wrong products being fed, products running out—we had to take a comprehensive approach." This systematic approach, inspired by the real world feeding challenges experienced by SmartPak's Founder Becky Minard with her horse Westley, are what have made SmartPaks so popular with riders, growing at 10 times the industry growth rate for the past 10 years.

Just what is a SmartPak you ask? SmartPaks are custom-made, pre-measured daily dose Paks of a horse's supplements. They hold between one and seven supplements in each compartment, and are labeled with the horse's name for fast and accurate feeding every time. Tightly sealed for 100 percent potency, SmartPaks ensure each horse always has the freshest supplements available. They are automatically delivered every month

straight to the barn so that you don't run out. By taking a systematic approach that combines unit dose packaging, mass-customization, content partnerships with all the leading supplement brands,

revolutionize

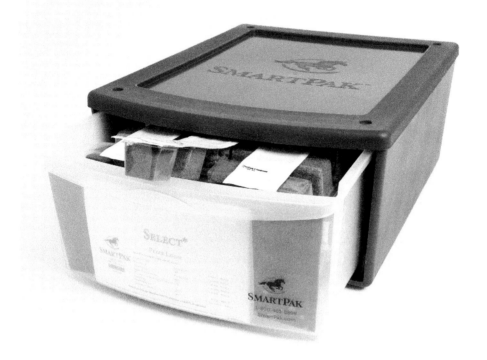

easy online management, and automatic replenishment, SmartPaks solve the supplement feeding problem systematically and completely. As its customers say, "SmartPaks simplify your life and provide a daily dose of peace of mind in a handy, compact size."

But it's not just the functionality of the SmartPak delivery system that has made the company the #1 equine e-commerce website. It's also the emotional connection to the rider. As a trusted health brand built on deep customer insights and first-hand research, SmartPak Equine has become a Lovemark to its customers (who sometimes refer to SmartPak as the Zappos of equine e-commerce). Here's commentary straight from SmartPak's customers (who range from young girls with their first pony to Olympic medalists):

"Dear SmartPak: I am in awe. My expectations for customer service have gotten pretty low in recent years, and so I've always been pleased with your great service and the fact that the little touches, like the welcoming phone call to me and my herd, really make the SmartPak experience special.

But I am in shock at how extremely kind you have been to me upon hearing, via the cancellation of one part of my regular shipment, of my horse Meg's death. I thought the personal e-mail was incredibly nice, but when I received a handwritten sympathy card today, mentioning Meg by name, I was stunned. OK, I cried. But it was the tears that come when you are in grief and someone shows you they care. One word: wow.

SmartPak customer service is way above and beyond just "customer service." You are truly special, wonderful, caring people and it matters SO much to me that you took the time to show this bit of concern. Even my vet didn't show this much care!

Thank you, thank you, thank you. Knowing I'm dealing with real people, who truly do understand not just the joy of equine ownership, but also the attendant grief that is ultimately inevitably a part of it, is truly invaluable.

I'm so touched that I don't know what to say or do—other than to assure you that I am telling every horse, donkey and mule owner I know about the extra special person-to-person care from what many would assume is "just a faceless, nameless internet company." Oh no—you are much, much more.

Very gratefully,"

Gisholt shares, "At SmartPak, everything we do is to help our customers have more quality time to spend with their horses. Horses are their first loves. We get that. We're here to make sure their horses stay healthy and they have plenty of riding time together."

ThinkAbout: REVOLUTIONIZE

Can a "systems thinking" approach revolutionize your product development efforts? How can you synch up and simplify all the links in one of your processes and solve a problem in your industry that others deem too tough to tackle? Do any of your products provoke the kind of Lovemark reactions that SmartPak's do?

*t*rue confessions: I used to buy Girl Scout Thin Mints *by the case* from an adorable young Girl Scout at our church. She'd sneak the case to me (we are only a family of two!) and I'd slip it into my car before someone in the congregation could think of the word gluttony. She's now in medical school (no doubt her early Girl Scout sales savvy and training has been an asset!), and now I have to dole out my purchases in smaller, less conspicuous amounts to girls standing in front of our various supermarkets in town.

I have been a blissful Thin Mint consumer for decades. I thought I knew all there was to know about these cookies and the girls behind them until I saw the organization's new "brand refresh" on its cookie packaging. It's one of the best examples of excellent short and simple storyselling I've seen. It succinctly tells and sells the story in clear cut copy and visuals.

As you may know, the girls primarily handsell these boxes door-to-door. The $3.50 is exchanged and the customer goes on her merry way to eat the two rows (one row per serving!). Now, while she is enjoying these cookies, she can look at the new box design and learn the following eight things:

- What girls in scouting do
- Stories in the girls' voices
- The real Girl Scout story
- Their sustainability efforts
- Further online info
- How to reconnect with the Girl Scouts
- The 5 skills girls learn from the product sale
- The cookies' deliciousness

This new packaging design truly advances the brand mission of the Girl Scouts. It's a touchpoint that no doubt helped the scouts sell 215 million of these boxes last year, adding up to $790 million worth of cookie sales. "We have more than 50 million cookie customers across the country, and the cookie box is the most tangible and powerful way for us to communicate directly with consumers," said Girl Scouts of the USA Chief Executive Officer Anna Maria Chávez. "So it's no surprise that our new cookie package tells the story of the five skills girls learn from participating in the cookie program. We want people to know that with each purchase of Girl Scout Cookies, they are not just getting a delicious treat, they are helping girls to be future business leaders and to make a difference in their communities."

P.S. The STORYSELLING continues!

If most Thin Mint lovers are like me, they are sad when their last box (or case!) is empty and the wait begins until the following year when they can replenish their stock. The smart leaders of the Girl Scouts decided to do something about that merchandising gap. They united with candy

powerhouse Nestlé and co-created an offering of three Nestlé Crunch Girl Scout Candy Bars to help commemorate their 100th anniversary. Here's what Barry Horowitz, vice president and general manager, Girl Scout Merchandise, Girl Scouts of the USA said at the time:

> "We're pleased that with the help of a great brand like Nestlé Crunch, our iconic Girl Scouts brand can reach the public in new and unexpected places. During our 100th anniversary, we hope the Nestlé Crunch Girl Scout Candy Bars raise awareness of the Girl Scout Cookie Program and all the business and financial literacy skills girls learn from participating in this annual leadership activity."

See just what can happen when you sell your story so well?

storysell

ThinkAbout: STORYSELL

How effectively are you telling and selling your product story
at its point of sale? How might your product sales benefit from
a more enhanced emotional storyselling approach?

*a*fter graduating from college I thought I wanted to open my own bookstore. Mitchell Kaplan, a friend, mentor, and owner of one of the nation's best independent bookstores, Books & Books, gave me excellent advice, "Go work at one first." I did just that and found myself working as a book buyer at a quaint shop in Old Town Alexandria, Virginia, for a season. One of my favorite memories of that time was handselling books. It was sheer joy to literally put books into people's hands and connect writers with readers.

Pleasant Rowland's book series for young girls had just come out. It's a series of historical books that follow a young girl's life through an accurate representation of a particular time period. Rowland, a former schoolteacher, called her company The Pleasant Company and her series, The American Girl Collection. It was so fun to introduce aunts and grandmas and moms to this wholesome, educational, and entertaining reading material for the young girls in their lives. After reading these first books, the 7 to 12 year olds would come into the store themselves, eagerly wondering if the next book in the series had hit the shelves.

Very soon after that, Rowland brought historically accurate dolls to market based on each of the book characters, complete with clothing and accessories. The stories and the dolls were all created to glorify girlhood in a very positive way. In an interview long ago about how the company was founded, Rowland shared this: "Mothers were tired of the sexualization of little girls, tired of making children grow up too fast. They yearned for a product that would both capture their child's interest and allow little girls to be little girls for a little longer." (Soon, those same girls would come into the bookstore carrying their dolls to purchase the next book!)

Indeed, the entire American Girl brand has been focused on this very mission:

> Helping girls become their very best. At American Girl, we celebrate girls and all that they can be. That's why we develop products and experiences that help girls grow up in a wholesome way, while encouraging them to enjoy girlhood through fun and enchanting play.

Glorifying the girlhood experience—past, present, and future—is what focuses the product developers at American Girl. The brand and product

glorify

Meet the American Girl historical characters

1764 — Meet Kaya
A daring Nez Perce girl

1812 — Meet Caroline
A brave girl growing up
during the War of 1812

1824 — Meet Josefi
A hopeful New Mex

1853 — Meet Marie-Grace & Cécile
Newfound friends
from New Orleans

1864 — Meet Addy
A courageous girl
from the Civil War era

Meet Rebe
A lively g
with drama

1934 — Meet Kit & Ruthie
Resourceful girls growing up
during the Great Depression

1944 — Meet Molly & Emily
Patriotic girls from the
World War Two era

1974 — Meet Julie & Ivy
Optimistic girls in
times of change

line has grown immensely since Rowland's start. Now a division of Mattel, American Girl still encompasses historically based books and dolls and accessories, but also experiential retail stores, complete with restaurants and doll hair salons, a magazine, and a website chockfull of games and interactivity. Each product is meticulously created to honor the girlhood experience and to have aunts, grandmothers, godmothers, mothers, and their daughters and nieces feel in their hearts, "It's good to be a girl."

ThinkAbout: GLORIFY

In what ways do your products honor your customers?
Do you have a relentless focus on glorifying an aspect of your customers' lives that your competitors just can't duplicate?
Are you proud of the products your brand delivers? As American Girl did with books and dolls, are there two unique products you can connect in some meaningful way?

S teve Leveen, Co-Founder and CEO of Levenger, a multichanneler retailer whose purpose is to inspire productivity and enhance customers' experiences as readers, writers, and thinkers, believes that "pens are portals to literacy. Holding a pen in our hand helps awaken our creative spirit and connect us to thoughts, aspirations and dreams. *Connect* is a verb we take seriously at Levenger."

Mim Harrison, Brand Strategist for Levenger, outlines what happens when their customers choose its beautiful True Writer fine writing instrument.

"Look at all the many different levels on which it helps you connect:

With yourself. What was once the quest for a work-life balance is now the search for ways to balance the virtual and the physical. 'Only connect,' said the novelist E.M. Forster, long before 'connectivity' was a word. Sometimes the best way we connect with ourselves is to temporarily disconnect from our electronics. Pen and paper become a quiet refuge.

With ideas. A pen is the physical extension of the hand-to-brain connection. Pick up a pen to put down your thoughts . . . sketch a scenario . . . jot a quick note . . . record the most meaningful parts of a presentation (your hand and your pen act as natural filters of the extraneous material). Or simply to doodle, which is its own type of mental gymnastics.

With an object of beauty. The protean nature of the resin barrel lends itself to waves of prismatic color. The object stays the same, but the beauty is ever-evolving.

With others. A handwritten note speaks to the recipient with a power that eludes electronic equivalents. As the author Stacy Schiff says, 'text and e-mail messages are of this world, a letter an attempt, however illusory, to transcend it.' The more scarce that handwritten notes are, the more cherished they become.

With your heritage. Pens are intrinsically connected to the heritage technology of paper. And it was by putting pen to paper that humans made the momentous shift from an oral culture to a written one: a culture of law, philosophy—and books."

These beloved writing instruments inspired a Levenger customer to connect even more deeply with this product . . . she wrote a poem about it!

connect

ThinkAbout: CONNECT

Does your product connect with your customer's soul?
Are their deeper levels of expression that you may have left
untapped? What emotional triggers can you explore for
a more intimate product experience?

Sheryl Clark, President of Boston Proper, a leading direct-to-consumer retailer of women's high-end apparel and accessories, knows that her customers want something different in their closets. "We've built our brand around designing styles that are daring, sophisticated and sensuous. Our customers like to wear things like no one else, and our goal as merchants is to inspire this independence in a fearless and feminine way."

When Boston Proper presents a functional travel wardrobe, for example, it is no run-of-the-mill boring and bland outfit. They know that "a perfect departure and arrival includes feeling good and looking even better." Clark and her team of designers and merchants showcase a complete Travel Collection with flair. Even their "basics" are not basic. Jackets, pants, tops and dresses all have just a little something extra. For example, take a look at the wrinkle free, figure-flattering, stretch, X-back travel dress with a square neckline and hear just what her customers have to say:

> "Perfect fitting! This dress packs well. Got to love the back! Very cute! A must have."

> "I've worn this dress once so far and love it. It fits well, is very flattering, and can be worn to the office and then out for the evening afterwards. The best feature, of course, is being able to wash and wear without requiring ironing or dry cleaning."

> "I travel quite a bit and always think of taking this dress. It's versatile, non-wrinkle and has a cute back detail. Great value!"

Boston Proper offers unique and distinctive fashion for today's independent, confident and active woman. They understand that each and every item in their customers' closets matters in defining their personal style. "A special stitch, a touch of sparkle or a subtle cutout gives our customer the confidence that she is indeed, wearing it like no one else."

Their customers are enviable and chic. They enjoy differentiating themselves through on-trend, age-appropriate fashions that enhance their femininity. Fiercely loyal to the unique collection, Boston Proper is their go-to source for these clothes.

differentiate

ThinkAbout: DIFFERENTIATE

Is one of your products a "basic" that needs some form of differentiation? How can you reinvent a bread-and-butter item into an essential "must have?" What twist can you add to a bestselling favorite so you can turn your customers' heads?

*h*ave you ever had one of those days? A really woolly day that tries your patience and uses up your last ounce of energy? The brand builders at Dayspring, the nation's premier Christian greeting card company, know all about those kinds of days. Twenty years ago, they had a vision to "connect people with the heart of God through messages of hope and encouragement every day, everywhere" with products that made real connections on an emotional level. Products that expressed care and concern, products that celebrated joy and blessings.

Dayspring's best-selling card line of all time, Really Woolly, created by Rose Mary Harris, anchored their foray into this category. Like all of us, Harris has had her fair share of really woolly days and understands the need for an uplifting word. The cards are based on real life situations and use whimsical illustrations (by artist Julie Sawyer) of sheep and often humorous copy to bring a smile or a word of encouragement to the recipient.

This is how Harris signs the back of the Really Woolly card collection:

"Life is Really Woolly! I know mine has been and I bet yours is too. That's why I love helping create these *Shepherd's-with-us* cards—so in the woolliest of times, you'll know the heartiest of care . . . His."

As concept designer and writer of this line, Harris shared this: "For most people, verbalizing and sharing our feelings with one another—whether good or not-so-good—can be hard. I created this line of cards to give people the words (via our fluffy sheep) to say what is in their hearts. I purposefully wrote the copy in a down-to-earth tone, no fluffy,

verbalize

pie-in-the-sky God-speak or "Christianese," but just friend-to-friend everyday language."

Based on Really Woolly's success at meaningfully articulating life's inflection points, the greeting card line has been expanded into gifts and children's products.

ThinkAbout: VERBALIZE

How well do your products articulate your brand's purpose? Do your products give voice to your customers' deeper needs or desires? If your products could talk, what would they say to your customers? Can you verbalize the emotions your customers experience in using your products?

"   es!" That's the first thing my husband and I said when we discovered our first pair of KEEN sandals nearly a decade ago one summer in an independent sporting goods store in Creede, Colorado. This sandal was like no other we had ever seen. It had a rugged bottom that allowed for hiking but wouldn't mar up sailboats. YES! It was happy to get wet (what we later learned was "washable polyester webbing upper with Aegis microbe shield™ which also means "no odor"!) but it was happy on trails too. YES! It had a comfortable, supported footbed. YES! But what really caught our attention was its unusual looking big black rubber toe guard. Ugly but effective. YES! (If you've ever stubbed your toe on sailboat hardware or slippery mountain stream rocks, you'll understand why this is so important.)

"Yes!" we said and enthusiastically each bought a pair. We now own several colors and have convinced most of our friends to wear them too. These sandals have gone everywhere with us and are often the only shoes we pack for adventure travel—from Colorado stream crossings to Hawaiian outings on lava rock to white Fijian beaches to Amalfi coastal hikes in Italy. They're even washable. YES!

KEEN is a YES company. It's a company that does not take no for an answer and its "yes we can" attitude permeates its entire brand and product line. KEEN calls this a "HybridLife:"

We all live many lives splitting our time between work, play, and giving back. At KEEN we call this living a HybridLife. HybridLife is the KEEN mantra, our commitment to create solutions in our product and business practices, to design footwear, bags and socks that enable you to play anyplace without a ceiling; and our promise to care for each other and the world around us. We invite you to join us in tossing on a pair of KEEN shoes, socks or a bag and to diving head first into living a HybridLife.

yes

CNX LIGHTWEIGHT PROTECTION FOR BRAVE NEW TOES.

MEN

WOMEN

KIDS

#BRAVENEWTOES

WATCH VIDEO

Yes is a verb that underscores its HybridLife philosophy and pushes KEEN to think "and" not "either/or." It's a verb that challenges the merchants and product developers to say "yes, we can make that sandal even better." And, that's just what they did with the advent of its new CNX technology: "We've shaved an entire line of footwear down to 10 oz. each, but kept the protection that made us famous. It's addition by subtraction." Their seriously playful campaign is called "Brave New Toes." YES!

ThinkAbout: YES

Does a YES! mindset permeate your product development process? What barriers might be keeping you from fully embracing a YES! attitude? What solutions have you created for your customers so that they can respond with a wholehearted YES! to your offering? Do you need to borrow KEEN's "addition by subtraction" philosophy for product enrichment?

*e*ileen Spitalny and David Kravetz are smart marketers. As childhood friends and co-founders of Fairytale Brownies, a Phoenix-based, direct-to-consumer gourmet food company, they have devoted the last 20+ years of their lives to being in the enchantment business.

I had the joy of experiencing their brand of enchantment firsthand when they invited me into Fairyland. It starts when you first walk in their door and smell the Fairytale Brownies being baked in the company's kitchen. Then you begin to notice the purposeful purple passion of their packaging while a Fairytale team member educates you on the plethora of brownie options (from signature Fairytale Brownies to snack-size Fairytale Sprites to bite-size Magic Morsels to classic Fairytale Cookies in all sorts of flavors) as you nibble on a delicious hard-to-choose-just-one Callebaut Belgian chocolate brownie. You just smile. You have tasted pure enchantment. You become a repeat customer. You are then genuinely thanked and encouraged to "Have a Fairytale day!"

"Enchantment is built into all our products," Kravetz shared. "It's an integral part of our planning process. We don't want to do ordinary. Our brownies aren't ordinary. Our packaging and our service aren't ordinary. We think through every aspect of every product and ask, 'How can this be even more enchanting?'"

Spitalny showed me their popular gift, the Photo Tin Medley. "We carefully created this to have lasting appeal. We want the enchantment factor to linger even after our brownies are eaten. This tin is decorated with our magical stars and cocoa vines and packed full of the highest quality brownies. And then we go a step further and personalize it with a favorite photo so that an even more meaningful emotional connection is made between the gift-giver and the recipient." (This photo happens to feature Eileen's daughter and dog.) Spitalny and Kravetz concurred: "Yes, our tagline, 'A Taste of Pure Enchantment' informs all that we do."

enchant

ThinkAbout: ENCHANT

Every product can benefit from a bit of fairy dust.
How can you wave an enchantment wand over your product?
What more can you do to make it even more
emotionally appealing?

$\mathcal{W}$hat kind of Christmas tree did you put up this year? An "old school" live version cut down at a farm or more handily, picked up at the Costco parking lot? Was it a Fraser fir? A grand noble? A blue spruce? Or, did yours come from a box, possibly even pre-lit? Whatever version is your tradition, no doubt it brought you joy. That's usually what traditions do.

But, did it beguile you? Was it conversation-worthy? Remarkable? Memorable? Unexpected?

For that tree, you may have had to go to Hammacher Schlemmer, America's longest running catalog. Hammacher Schlemmer is in the beguiling business. Offering "the Best, the Only, and the Unexpected since 1848," you could have charmed not only your family, but all your friends and holiday visitors with an exclusive Fashionista Christmas Tree (for just $249.95). Here's the scoop:

> The Fashionista Christmas Tree eschews the geometric lines of typical trees and is tailored to the shape of a three-dimensional mannequin, a form more common to department store windows and fashion designers' studios. The dark-green needles wrap tightly around the high collar, along the torso and arms, and across the hoop skirt, evoking memories of traditional Christmas conifers while accentuating the curves of the dress form. It is pre-strung with 150 LEDs that glimmer through the evergreen foliage from the shapely torso past the perfect size-four waist, and eight removable, iridescent globe ornaments cast a ruby-red hue while leaving room for personal holiday trimmings.
>
> "The Fashionista Christmas Tree allows one to celebrate the holiday season in an elegant, fashionable manner, while still providing a way to display traditional Christmas decoration," explained Hammacher Schlemmer's General Manager Fred Berns.

Who would have thought you could tinker with a 15th-century tradition and change the shape of the tree? The Hammacher Schlemmer merchants specialize in entertainment thinking. The Fashionista Christmas Tree is just one of the many intriguing items you'll find as you wander with child-like awe through the rest of their product offerings (don't miss the $50,000 Barbeque Dining Boat or, if budget is a factor, the $42,000 Hot Tub Boat). This is retailing at its finest.

beguile

ThinkAbout: BEGUILE

What would happen if your product went to charm school?
How can you take what already exists or is expected and turn
it into something more entertaining? More remarkable? More
beguiling? What twist on tradition can you add to your product?

*t*erri Alpert founded multichanneler Uno Alla Volta to offer her customers treasures and collectibles that they would cherish. *Uno Alla Volta* is Italian for "one at a time" and these items are handpicked by Alpert and her team of merchants because they are indeed handcrafted one at a time in a labor of love to beautify, inspire, and touch the soul.

"Yes, we believe these objects from the hearts and hands of artisans need to be cherished but let me tell you how we cherish the process of creation every step of the way," says Alpert. "We honor the human creativity and individuality behind each product. We know our artists and their stories. There are traditions behind our products and within them memories of the spirit of the person who created them. Take our Glass Torsade Necklace by Giulio for an example:

> In his Castella studio, just a short walk from Venice's famed St. Mark's Square, Giulio continues the lampwork tradition of his grandmother. Each of the thousands of beads in this stunning jewel-toned torsade necklace, is handmade, uno alla volta, over a small flame.

These beads reflect our artisan's creativity, his home town of Venice, and his love of his grandmother. We are the caretakers of this story. We share this with our customers so that they too can value and appreciate these beads in a deeper way. We firmly believe that treasures like this deserve to be cherished and it is our job at Uno Alla Volta to connect the work of our artisans with customers who want to become caretakers of these items."

Alpert knows all of this intuitively and it is the guiding mission of her company. But recently she surveyed her customers with this question: "When you know that a creation was made as a labor of love by a fellow human being, does that change your relationship with the treasure?" The feedback was an overwhelming, "Yes, definitely. I am the creation's caretaker."

"It's clear to us: we are *all* in the cherishing business—our merchants, our artists, our customers!" beams Alpert.

cherish

ThinkAbout: CHERISH

Do you give your customers reason to cherish the products your brand creates? Why or why not? What might you do to link the passion behind your product with your customers' experience of your product? How might simple storytelling become an effective brand enhancer?

*f*or 20+ years, the merchants at Tommy Bahama have asked one clarifying question as they created a brand "that elevated relaxation to a fine art" and that question is "What Would Tommy Do?" Tommy's identity is even a tab on the website:

The Legend

Known for his charm, wit and perpetual tan, Tommy Bahama embodies the island life. An intrepid traveler, he speaks nine languages fluently and can flirt in dozens more. Once, he caught a 200-pound yellowfin using only a coconut shell, some broken sunglasses and the drawstring from his swim trunks.

The Truth

The legendary Tommy Bahama is just that: A legend, a personification of an

idyllic life. Inspired by the refined, unhurried attitude of coastal life, our founders created the character to define the very essence of our brand. Even today, we let our fictional namesake's debonair lifestyle guide almost every decision.

As the product developers at Tommy Bahama create a varied assortment of island-inspired goods and services to "Make Life One Long Weekend," they do so through this filter that simplifies, focuses and concentrates their efforts. "What kind of cologne would Tommy wear?" (See several options depending on his mood: TB for Him, Set Sail for Martinique, Signature, St. Bart's and Vintage Paradise.) "What kind of bike would he cruise around the island on?" (One with an electric motor of course . . . no stress!) "What cocktail would Tommy drink at his restaurant's island happy hour?" (Perhaps a Painkiller #2 or a Bahama Mama!) Asking these questions internally and creatively and collaboratively answering them together as part of the merchants' decision-making process leads to products and services that have an authenticity that makes people forget that Tommy Bahama is but a legend.

The "What Would Tommy Do?" filter has led to other brand-enhancing decisions such as creating a National Relaxation Day (August 15)

filter

Tommy Bahama

MAKE LIFE *one* LONG WEEKEND

In a world of schedules and to-do lists, the ability to relax and enjoy life is becoming a lost art. We're wise to the ways of the good life. So get inspired and see our favorite photos, watch a video or learn more about the legend of Tommy Bahama.

Whether you want to learn how to hula, or even mix one of our island-time cocktails, we invite you to be a guest in our virtual paradise. And, if you're ready to live the dream, consider joining our team.

Never before has it been so easy to dig your toes in the virtual sand and make life one long weekend.

or Island Email or placing Recipes for Island Cocktails on its website and even video clips about "How to Hula" featuring one of their online merchants. The Tommy Bahama filter is an important lens that does not constrain, but rather serves to allow more creative merchandising and brand sunshine in. Tommy, no doubt, would approve of this filter process!

ThinkAbout: FILTER

What filter are you using as your products/services fit chart? How does this filter focus your merchandising energy and provoke brand-wide conversations? Perhaps your filter is intuitive and not formally documented. Would it be helpful to formalize it in some way?

ohn Vitek, President of Saint Mary's Press, a contemporary curriculum publisher of religious educational materials, believes Bibles are meant to be read not shelved; studied, prayed through, and lived out, not left unopened. He and the Saint Mary's Press team have a knack for creating Bibles that people want to read. Years ago, they pioneered a whole new approach to Bibles that engaged the fickle teen market and went on to become an industry bestseller (The Catholic Youth Bible). They did it again for middle-schoolers (Breakthrough Bible) and then again for college students (Anselm Academic Study Bible). And, because parents were "borrowing" their kids' Bibles, they created one for entire families (The Catholic Family Connections Bible).

But it's this latest Bible, the Catholic Children's Bible, for second through fourth graders, for which Vitek has great enthusiasm. "This was uncharted territory for us. We never created a Bible before for this young of a reader. Our challenges were great. I am so proud of the process that the multi-disciplinary team at Saint Mary's Press utilized in connecting with these beginning readers and their learning styles. The end product totally captures the imaginations of these young readers. The kids are WOWED! They love that they can actually read the Bible firsthand, not have someone read it to them. How empowering is that?" Vitek said.

EMPOWER. It's a key brand driver for all the products created by this innovative publisher. The verb is right there in the first line of its product launch copy:

> It's the first-ever complete children's Bible that not only inspires, but *empowers* children to read, live, understand, and love the Word of God. The stories come alive with vivid, awe-inspiring artwork, larger text, and many more design features that not only enhance comprehension but create enjoyment as well.

Heather Sutton, Associate Publisher, oversaw the comprehensive, user-centered experience that guided this product's creation. "We started by sitting in on second grade classrooms and just watching the teachers interact with the kids. We paid attention to what worked, what didn't; where the kids got bored, where they got excited. It was fascinating! Then

empower

we brought in an advisory board of outside experts—teachers, artists, writers—to teach us more. All of this listening and learning translated into components that empower children to read this Bible on their own. Intentional editorial elements (such as sentence length, word choice) design elements (such as font choices in sizes that assist early readers, one column text when possible instead of two, increased line spacing, bold vocabulary words, colorized text, minimal hyphenation) and unique navigational features (such as colorized tabs, large chapter and verse numbers, full Scripture references, and clear and concise story titles) as well as our iPad app, make this Bible well built for early readers and were done to make this Bible become, we hope, one of their all-time favorite childhood books."

ThinkAbout: EMPOWER

Creating empowering products is a privilege. How does your product empower your customers? How can you go "back to school" on one of your products and find ways to possibly make it even more empowering for your customers?

*m*ost parents are thrilled to hear a teacher report that their child "plays well with others." For Matt Glerum, President and CEO of TravelSmith, an upscale multichanneler of "clothing, gear and advice to go," his customers are thrilled when all his products "travel well with others."

"Physically how a product travels is of utmost importance to us," he says. "It's our guiding brand principle and it's what our customers depend on from us. Our merchants know exactly what travelers need—they are seasoned travelers themselves. They curate an assortment of the best possible clothing, luggage, and travel gear for our customers. TravelSmith clothing often needs to do double and possibly triple wardrobe duty and look great after being stuffed in a suitcase for a week or worn on the redeye overnight."

Glerum shares, "Two products that really tell our brand story are the Crinkle Fiesta Skirt for women and the Hybrid Travel Jacket for men. They both demonstrate the duality of product function and flattery!"

Crinkle Fiesta Skirt

We've expanded the sizing on this customer favorite so it looks good on everyone. Our great travel skirt has tiers of crinkles that disguise wrinkles and swirls of embellishment for even more visual interest. Its myriad colors match almost every top you own, so it will most likely spend more time on you than in the included travel pouch. Elastic drawstring waist. Fully lined. 100% cotton. Machine wash.

travel

Men's Hybrid Travel Jacket

Travel is unpredictable, which is why you need this coat. Re-styled with an updated fit, it's smart enough to wear to a casual dinner, packable enough to toss in a duffel and rugged enough to handle the outdoors. What's more, this coat's soft microfiber drapes and feels like sueded silk but resists water and wrinkles. Ten pockets, including two security pockets, hold everything. Hidden interior back-waist draw cord. Fully lined. Relaxed fit. Poly-nylon. Machine wash cold.

But what really matters is how TravelSmith's customers feel about these clothes. Here are two stories straight from their travels:

"I own three of the Men's Hybrid Travel Jackets, one in Navy, one in Tan, and my most recent one in Olive. They are absolutely great for travel. My Navy version is the oldest and has done the most traveling to Europe, South America and most recently to China. As a researcher, I have worn them to make formal presentations at national and international meetings and to go to places where coat and tie are required. They are a very practical item that is easy to pack or to wear on a plane. The Men's Hybrid Travel Jacket is an essential part of my travel wardrobe. I don't leave home without one."

"WOW! When I read the other reviews I thought nothing could be this great. Was I ever wrong!!! This has got to be the best item I've ever had from TravelSmith & I've been buying from TravelSmith for over 12 years. I wore the skirt for the first time a few days ago & after reading the reviews, I took a note pad with me so I could be prepared to give out TravelSmith's website. In a couple hours of shopping & lunching, I only was stopped 7 times & 5 of the people asked where I got the skirt. I've never had this happen before in my entire life and I'm over 50. I may have to print some business cards next time I go out in this skirt!"

ThinkAbout: TRAVEL

Most product developers would be thrilled to have their products travel along with their customers each and every day. How can you make your product more "travel-worthy"? Do any of your products do double or triple duty in some way? What kinds of stories are traveling along with your product?

i wrote about the wonder and power of Etsy in my first book, *Brand-About*. The delightful website that connects craftsmanship with commerce and gives artisans (whether paper crafters or beadmakers or fine artists or knitters or woodworkers) a place to share their hand-crafted goods and the stories behind them not just with local customers, but literally with the world.

For a multitude of reasons, the days of moms and dads or grand-mas and grandpas passing down their cooking or quilting or furni-ture-building talents seem to be van-ishing. But our desire to learn these skills or apprentice under someone have not waned. Craftsy fills this bill.

Craftsy describes itself as:

> [A] community of people who love to make things. We Knit. We Quilt. We Crochet. We Make Jewelry. We Sew. We Decorate. We're Creative. We're Unique. We're learning from, inspir-ing and helping each other. We are dedicated to providing the best edu-cation and resources for crafters.

MAKE. On the surface it's such a simple four letter verb. But when was the last time you actu-ally made something from scratch, by hand, by yourself? We just might thinkabout MAKE more than we actually ever make MAKE happen! Well, enter Craftsy. The online learning environment that *gets* busy people and understands just what kind of classes they need to make things happen. Their approach is fun, helpful, and interactive.

Here's just one example of their Food Craft product offerings: How to Make a Perfect Pizza at Home by Peter Reinhart:

Learn how to make pizza in this fresh, flavorful, FREE mini-class with baking guru Peter Reinhart! Stretch your dough and your imagination as Peter guides you through each step of making a pizza. You'll make pizza sauces, consider cheese options and bake five types of dough in your conventional home oven. Impress Italian purists with a slice of your Sicilian-style, homemade pies, provide your gluten-free pizza lovers with mouth-watering meals or cook creative flavor combinations for more adventurous palates.

And here are just two pieces of feedback (from over 5,000 pizza students who took this course):

"I followed the American Style Napolitana recipe—made it for kid's birthday at our place. We had an Italian parent who said when he saw the first pizzas coming out of the oven: 'This looks like real Napolitana—what kind of oven do you have?!!!' We could not stop eating: perfect crust, light, thin and at the same time airy with wonderful air pockets at the edges, so you don't feel like your stuffing yourself with a baked piece of dough. Thank you, Chef!"

"What a great class! Chef Reinhart provided all of the information I needed to make some great pizzas on the first go (in fact, I made a party out of it with some friends). It was clear he was incredibly knowledgeable, and he kept me interested. The detail that went into describing how to work the dough was especially helpful, as I had never made a yeasted dough before and was a little scared that I would totally mess it up."

Craftsy enabled these students to make something that they had never attempted before. All by themselves. What a powerful verb! Craftsy may be just the training ground for the next generation of Etsy sellers.

make

Cooking | **Online Classes** | **Patterns** | **Projects** | **Supplies** | *Blog*

At a Glance

6 HD Video Lessons

REVIEWS

★ ★ ★ ★ ★

INSTRUCTOR

Peter Reinhart

A baking instructor at Johnson & Wales University and TED Talks speaker. Peter is also the author of five bread baking books, including *The Bread Baker's Apprentice.* View profile »

Perfect Pizza at Home

with Peter Reinhart

Learn how to make pizza in this fresh, flavorful, FREE mini-class with baking guru Peter Reinhart!

Overview   Lessons   Materials   Reviews
—————

Stretch your dough and your imagination as Peter guides you through each step of making a pizza. You'll make pizza sauces, consider cheese options and bake five types of dough in your conventional home oven.

ThinkAbout: MAKE

What does your product make your customers do? Is there an addition (or a subtraction!) to your product line that might motivate them further? What's your recipe for making your products an integral part of your customers' lives?

o you happen to recollect a Silver Tinsel Tree like this one from your Christmases past? The merchants at The Vermont Country Store rediscovered it and describe it this way:

Remember the silvery tinsel trees from the 50s and 60s, so shiny, so wonderfully unnatural, so full of sparkle and light? So many of our customers wanted to re-create that magical look that we found them, complete with bursts of feathery soft, silvery plastic needles.

"Made my mom cry" are not words a company usually wants to hear about one of their products, unless you are one of the merchants and brand leaders at The Vermont Country Store, and you know the customer means cry in a *good* way! Referring to this Silver Tinsel Tree, the customer elaborated:

"My mom had a tree like this growing up. She has talked about it all of my life. She cried when she opened the present on Christmas morning. She was so happy."

Chris Vickers, President and CEO, says his team is used to this. "Our products have been known to sometimes cause 'good' tears! We really are in the 'remind' business. Our products remind you of a person or a place or a time gone by. Our products also remind all of us that simpler is sometimes better and products that just plain work never go out of fashion. And, our products also remind our customers that it is OK for them to take some time out for themselves whether it is getting a new outfit, a treat to share with friends, or something that just helps them remember a good memory. We like being in the remind business."

The Vermont Country Store began in 1946 and still prides itself as the "purveyors of the practical and hard-to-find." Founded by the Orton family, this brand continues to be run with old-fashioned values and pride. Says Eliot Orton: "We still go to great lengths to find products that aren't sold anywhere else." Stroll through its New England-based general store in person or flip through one of its catalogs or linger on its website and The Vermont Country Store will remind you to experience the joy of a nostalgic trip down memory lane.

ThinkAbout: REMIND

Out of all your product offerings, which one reminds your customers most of your brand? Do any of your iconic products have subtle reminder possibilities tucked inside waiting to be leveraged? What positive associations do they evoke for your customers? Or, do they remind your customers of future opportunities? What attributes do you need to remind yourself about as you create new products that enhance your brand's positioning?

*W*hen Robin Sheldon, President and Founder of Soft Surroundings, launched her vision over 14 years ago, she purposefully wanted to create a soothing and inviting place for women to pamper themselves not only on special occasions, but also a place that encouraged them to live that way on a daily basis. Here's what she has to say:

> Busy women of all ages are our customers—especially those who need to be reminded to put themselves at the top of their "To Do List." Our philosophy is that by putting yourself first, you can take better care of friends and family and hopefully live a happier, more fulfilling life.
>
> We don't use the word "pamper" because wearing soft, comforting clothes, sleeping on fine linens and soothing your body and mind should be an everyday occurrence, something you owe yourself regularly—not just a treat.

Soft Surroundings tagline is "My Time. My Place. My Self." Just being on her site or in her stores feels like a retreat. A retreat you want to make happen right within your own home. After some nudging from her customers (they always wanted to purchase the store and catalog "props"), Sheldon and her team decided that was just what they wanted to do next. In order for their customers to fully create a "home as sanctuary" experience, the merchants and product developers decided they needed to launch a new home décor line. They called it RETREAT.

Sheldon elaborates: "For this new collection we immersed ourselves in the countryside of Provence. Bringing back antiques and artifacts, we used many of these pieces as design templates for the beautiful French reproduction furniture and vintage inspired decor that Soft Surroundings now offers. All of the pieces are made with quality craftsmanship, but are also very reasonably priced. Additionally, many of the original antiques are now available for sale on our site in a section called Brocante."

retreat

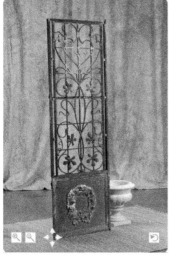

NARBONNE CHAPEL DOOR
$999.00

YOU MAY ALSO
LIKE...

Quantity 1

ADD TO BAG

This beautiful wrought iron chapel door is detailed with an intricate wreath design topped with a scrolling openwork heart motif. A stunning statement piece that brings rich texture wherever it's displayed. Circa 1900.
Please note:
Door has an additional delivery freight charge of $120.00.

Gilded Cornice
Trumeaux

▸ More product information

Rue Michelet Scale
Model

Here is just an example of what the merchants brought back from that trip: the Narbonne Chapel Door, described as "circa 1900 . . . a stunning statement piece that brings rich texture wherever it's displayed." Quite perfect for a home sanctuary!

Retreat, the verb that anchored their brand philosophy (soft being their brand adjective!), became a collection for Soft Surroundings and also a stand-alone catalog offer. Isn't it simply amazing what can happen when one takes a bit of time to herself to retreat?

ThinkAbout: RETREAT

Does your product development team need some time to themselves? Out of the fray? Out of the dailyness? Perhaps travelling out of the tried and true places of inspiration? What might happen if your team took a retreat to breathe deeply and look at your offering with fresh eyes? What hints have your customers been dropping that you may have ignored or put off for a multitude of reasons? Is it time to sit quietly with those whispers and listen to what they may be prompting you to do?

*f*or 35+ years, Rod's Western Palace has taken pride in being the source for everything Western—from Western apparel and tack to unique Western gifts and home décor. They have everything for the horse lover (whether you own horses, aspire to, or just admire them) and they can outfit your horse and stable as well. When one first thinks of "all things Western," bedding is not what pops to mind. But at Rod's Western Palace, the new Cowboy Paisley Quilted Bedding Collection in soft hues of spring green, cool blue, warm brown, and cream has scored high marks with its Western lifestyle customers.

Executive Vice President, Phil Minix, shares this: "What we are finding with our diverse brand is that our customers are looking to us to show them new trends and unexpected colorations that fit in with their Western lifestyle. In some ways, we are their "Western permission slip" brand that creatively shows them how to mix and match patterns, colors. We encourage and permit them to experiment more in fashion and home décor than our competitors. We want our customers to make our products truly their own. That's our unique point of view."

Karen Hartle, the merchant responsible for this best-selling collection, elaborates on this idea of permission: "As a company, we first had to give *ourselves* permission to think out of the box regarding bedding. It was a risk for us. We had plenty of quilts with classic Western imagery (horse, ranch motifs) but this quilt took us in a new direction. We were able to offer a very different look and showcase its Western appeal with coordinating pillows and room accessories. I believe the artfully decorated bedroom shot of this bedding really gave our customers permission to take Western to a new level in their own home. We opened up new decorating possibilities for them. They love that about us!"

RODS.com
TRUE WESTERN LIVING
Fashion • Gifts • Home • Tack

Rod's Permission Slip:
Enjoy the Western Lifestyle
in every part of your house,
even in your bedding!

permit

ThinkAbout: PERMIT

As a product developer, what might you need a
permission slip to do? Does your product grant your customer
permission to do something out of the ordinary?
How can your product props permit new possibilities?

*d*ave Bolotsky founded Uncommon Goods with the belief that "creativity and the expression of individuality represent two great human treasures. Our goal is to create business that makes uncommon goods accessible to everyone."

Here's a perfect example of how this works from its collection of artisan products:

State of the Art Map

Artist Aaron Foster takes you on a recycling road trip with a one-of-a-kind handmade license plate map of the USA. Each state is represented by an authentic license plate and mounted on a painted, cedar background, with Alaska and Hawaii included on separate boards. Each map is one-of-a-kind and the varied styles and never ending palette of America's old license plates allow for unlimited color combinations in his work. The license plate map of the United States was inspired partly from his collection of old globes and school maps that fill his eclectic home. Says Foster: "I always wonder about the history of the vintage plates I use . . . what roads they may have traveled down already and where they might be headed next."

Bolotsky says that *create* is an integral part of his brand's DNA. "Like many of our products, this license plate map supports our mission on many levels: it captures an element of history by repurposing the vintage license plates; the design creates both attractive art and a conversation piece. And, by having it as part of our selection of uncommon goods, we create a wider community for Foster's work. As a brand, we love to seek out independent artists and their creations and share them with a larger community. Our customers appreciate this authenticity!"

create

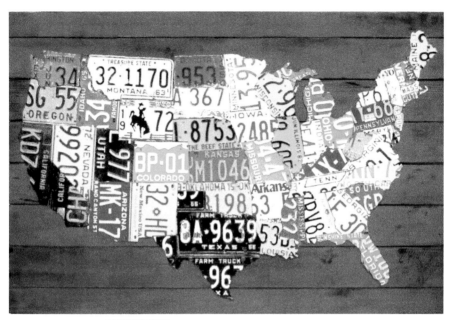

Here's one short but powerful customer's response to Foster's creation: "It is authentic. Awesome."

ThinkAbout: CREATE

Does your brand specialize in the unusual or uncommon?
What products have you created that would generate that
same customer response: "Awesome! Authentic!"?
How can you create conversation starters?

*f*or Springsteen fans simply getting a six disc (CDs and DVDs) boxed set was cause for celebration. But one that included a documentary, live performances, previously unreleased outtakes and an 80 page spiral bound reproduction of his original note-book with handwritten details of the recording sessions for the albums, alternate lyrics, song ideas, personal notes, an essay by Springsteen and never before seen photos, was like Christmas in a package. The only thing that could possibly top it was Springsteen sitting there opening it with you. *The Promise: The Darkness on the Edge of Town Story* deserved the Grammy it won for Best Boxed or Special Limited Edition Package.

Springsteen has always cared about the minute details of his lyrics, his performances and his listener relationships, but by bundling this extravaganza of intimate details together, he gives his fans a package that some describe, rightfully, as a "pièce de résistance." The 21 previously-unreleased songs speak for themselves, but the real fascination lies in the notebook as part of this package. Every page is a vignette into this troubadour's soul. His fans get a rare backstage pass to his creative process and get to see how his thoughts, fragments, and scribbles turn into songs. The scraps of paper, notes to himself, the posing of photos for possible covers, the playlists for various Jersey clubs, and the promo materials from some of those performances all taped together on spiral bound pages of an ordinary blue lined composition book, give his followers hours and hours of education and entertainment that only the Boss can deliver.

Most Springsteen aficionados already have every album he's made and possibly more (bootleg!); it's the packaging of all these components together that give this particular product its pizzazz. Springsteen fan Chris Lydon, VP, Enrollment Management & Marketing, Stonehill College

package

shared this: "For his longtime and exceedingly loyal fans, *The Promise* delivered a glimpse at the authentic Springsteen. We know the music and we rave about the live experience; but here, the curtain was pulled back to reveal what he was thinking, his creative perfectionism, and his journey to complete *Darkness on the Edge of Town*. It was an extraordinary gift that made the music itself even better the second time around."

ThinkAbout: PACKAGE

Are you holding anything back in your product packaging that your customers just might be interested in? Is your product packaging Grammy-worthy? What backstage "extras" might you consider adding to create an even more memorable product experience?

*t*here are the less is more brands. There are the more is less brands and there are the less is less brands. But, what would happen if you just zeroed out all the products in your store and simply offered your male shopper-who-really-isn't-thrilled-about-shopping a beer and some free advice? Guidance tailored to his particular body, his real-life clothing needs? Then, as he drank his beer, you brought him just the right amount of potential clothes to try on (just like Goldilocks would have preferred— not too many choices, not too few, for he has other things he'd like to do!). You made this process painless, easy and actionable by taking note of the options that not only fit but actually fit *well*. You record all these details, place an order online (his specific colors, cuts, washes, sizes) and send him home smiling and anticipating hanging these "just right" clothes in his closet in the next 48 hours. What if you gave customers the gift of guidance through all your product assortments with zero pressure, zero hassle, zero waste of time? Might that just be priceless?

Andy Dunn, founder of Bonobos, a "clothing brand focused on delivering great fit, high energy and superb customer service" believes that his indeed is a strategy that will lead to lots of zeroes. In an interview with *Bloomberg Enterprises*, he talked about the idea of "fitting for life" and really understanding his male shopper's needs. About the importance of new school "fit intelligence" paired with old school "fit ninjas" (Bonobos' term for their customer service experts) and focusing on making the entire shopping experience one of zero hassle. Bonobos calls these zero inventory places their Guideshops.

Erin Ersenkal, chief of Bonobos Guideshop operations shared this in a *USA Today* interview: "We founded Bonobos to really create a better shopping experience for men. Initially, we thought we could do it purely on a website,

zero

but we realized from talking to our customers that actually some of them like to try on the clothes." Guiding, helping, solving problems, not letting customers walk out with merchandise that might ultimately disappoint, remembering what worked and what didn't, recording fit intelligence to save time in the future. No doubt, the Bonobos male shopper certainly thinks that all this *less* is so much *more*.

ThinkAbout: ZERO

Look at your products through this zeroing lens:
what can you eliminate, erase, eradicate?
How might that exercise actually amplify your offer?
What guidance presently comes with your product or service?
What might be even more helpful?

*h*ave you ever played one of those games in a branding ideation session: If your brand was a car, what model would it be? If it was a color? A celebrity? A city? A holiday? While it's fun to conjecture clever responses, the real fruit of the exercise lies in the WHY. Why that color, why that celebrity? Is there a commonality in connecting all the answer dots that will lead your team to uncover the subtle nuances that set your brand apart?

The insightful folks at Kate Spade decided that their new brand launch to recruit a younger target audience would be best represented by the mindset of a weekend day: Saturday. As reported in *Women's Wear Daily,* "Kate Spade Saturday is priced about 50 percent below Kate Spade

New York. While both are colorful, bold, and optimistic collections, Kate Spade Saturday is geared to a younger customer about 25 to 35 years old, while Kate Spade New York targets women 30 to 40 years old and older."

Think of Kate Spade Saturday as Kate Spade New York's little sister. However, she doesn't have to borrow clothes from her big sister's closet; she's got her own whole wardrobe! These clothes are casual, comfy, and easy to wear with a bit of playfulness. (No doubt, her "older sister" might just want to borrow from her closet from time to time!)

Saturday.com's bright and bold website captures the spirit of just what makes this day unique from the other six:

No alarm clock

Best day ever

Letting your hair down

Choosing your own adventure

Just better than Tuesday

recruit

MAKE PLANS FOR SATURDAY.

A NEW BRAND FROM KATE SPADE NEW YORK IS LAUNCHING THIS SPRING.

By recruiting the "younger sisters" in their brand family with imaginative fashions, the Kate Spade team is smartly building their *next* 20+ year future.

ThinkAbout: RECRUIT

Pick a product from your repertoire. If this product was a day of the week, what day would it be and why? What associations might you make between that day and your product?
Are there new target audiences in your brand's future?
Or, could an existing product be repositioned in some way to pull in a new customer segment? How can your products help recruit future brand fans?

i like to pay special attention to brands that get me to adapt a new behavior. I know how very hard that is. For example, I had no real interest in yogurt. Yes, despite all the healthy benefits, I just couldn't muster up any yogurt love. Until my sister said, "Trust me. Try Chobani. It'll change your mind. It's not like all the other yogurts."

She was right. I am now a raving Chobani fan. This happened for many reasons but chief among them is the fact that this is a brand obsessed with absolutely every detail of its product line. It starts with the founder and CEO, Hamdi Ulukaya believing "there's an emotion to eating yogurt. You can make this a moment: the opening of it, the eating of it, the experience." A recent article in *Bloomberg Businessweek* tells the Turkish entrepreneur's story of obsessing over all the details involved in yogurt making. He simply wants to make yogurt as delicious as what his mom used to make when he was a child in eastern Turkey. If sales tell the story, I believe he's fulfilled that dream: Ulukaya, an independent businessman, will sell more than $1 billion of his yogurt in this upcoming year.

One of the many things I admire about Ulukaya is his roll-up–his-sleeves immersion into his products. He hasn't stopped innovating despite the fact that he's grown a niche category into a $6.5 billion market. He's obsessed with making yogurt "not boring" and turning more people like me into raving fans. Look at what "not boring" things he's done to yogurt this year alone:

Chobani Bites™

Tinier portions of yogurt to "help keep afternoon hunger pangs at bay and turn snacking into a mindful indulgence." With flavors like fig with orange zest and raspberry with dark chocolate chips, Ulukaya is bringing a gourmet mindset to this category.

Chobani Champions® Tubes

Designed so that no spoon is needed and "made to give kids authentic strained Greek low-fat yogurt to enjoy on-the-go."

obsess

Chobani Flip™

Customers were already adding health
mixings as they enjoyed their yogurt. In this product, Ulukaya did it for them—adding slice toasted almonds, oats, pecans, raspberries, and more!

Chobani Fan-Sourced Flavors: Pear and Banana

And, certain that he doesn't have all the answers, Ulukaya went straight to his customers and asked which two new flavors to add. Hands down, they told him: Pear and Banana!

ThinkAbout: OBSESS

What boring details are you NOT obsessing about that could lead to deeper product loyalty? What are you waiting for? Can you create new packages for your products to appeal to new audiences or to generate new consumption patterns with existing customers?

*h*ow many times has "I wonder what I'll wear this morning?" been your on-the-way-to-work conundrum? As an ultra-busy business professional, your early morning brain spins with all the sorts of details that await you at the office—the pitch that needs developing, the presentation that needs fine-tuning, the pending negotiation detail left to attend to. You just wish someone had laid out your clothes for the day so you'd have one less thing to think about!

Attention, men: you are in luck! Paul Fredrick, a direct-to-consumer retailer, offers "smart style for professional men." This brand specializes in presenting its male customers sophisticated and office-worthy combinations of suits, shirts, pants, and everything else needed to look and feel confident.

Lyle Croft, Executive VP Merchandising for Paul Fredrick, explains: "We have two types of customers: some don't have time at all to think through all the details of their wardrobe. They look to us to simplify that process and lay out the right combinations for them via our catalog and web presentations as well as through conversations with our experienced customer care representatives. Other men enjoy the art of combining patterns and prints themselves and look to us for encouragement on how to stand out a bit more. They appreciate our style sense and are delighted by our thoughtful and bold color-coordinated combinations. We really wardrobe the professional from head to toe," says Croft.

"Take a look at this combination. The color ways, the pattern plays, the coordinated variety of options really empower our men to dress smartly. That's our edge … we bring a detailed dressing room of options and a range of styles (from board-presentation-for-

wardrobe

Paul Fredrick

mal to casual-Friday-informal) to their fingertips. We put it all together for them in creative and innovative ways. What's truly rewarding for our merchants is that our customers tell us all the time about the compliments they receive on their clothing. So I guess you can say that Paul Fredrick is in the wardrobe compliment business!"

Wardrobing as a complete verb but with different meanings for each of its customer segments. It's what Paul Fredrick does best.

ThinkAbout: WARDROBE

Does your product line offer a head-to-toe complete solution for your customer? What's your wardrobe of conundrum solvers? Are your products garnering more compliments than your competitors'?

*t*he brand leaders at Guitar Center, the world's largest retailer of guitars, amplifiers, drums, keyboards and pro-audio and recording equipment, know that music is more than an enthusiast activity. Music brings people together. Chris Tso, Guitar Center's Vice President of Merchandising, explained, "Our mission is to help people make music—whether they play, perform or record. To do that, we invest a lot of our corporate resources (time, people, energy, and budget) on education. We help educate in several ways. One is by specializing in things like band instruments for sale and rental, serving teachers, band directors, parents, students, and an extensive national lesson program through our Music and Arts stores.

"Another one of our educational tools is our in-store "Recording Made Easy" program. We provide free recording workshops aimed at taking the complexity out of home recording. They are month-long classes with four weekly components averaging 2,000 registered attendees per week. We really want to demystify the process of creating music so people can enjoy and share their creations. In our "Recording Made Easy" sessions, musicians can take their ideas from basic tracks to finished songs by learning how to use Garageband on an Apple computer and Pro Tools (literally used by the pros!). It's exciting to watch people learn and grow."

Tso also mentioned another education program that has really gained interest—its free ukulele lessons on Saturday mornings all across the country. "We're excited about the interest we've had in these lessons from two areas—families and women; our customers normally skew heavily male. But the ukulele is actually a very simple gateway instrument to others. We're thrilled about the turnout at these lessons with about 1,000 registrants per week. The classes are fun, easy, and engaging and are part of our overall mission to educate and inspire."

educate

FREE UKULELE LESSONS

Every Saturday in April at 10:15 a.m. At Guitar Center*

REGISTER NOW

Without a doubt, over the past few years the ukulele has gained a stronger presence in popular music. The uke is a great addition to any player's arsenal, and an excellent way to get started for new musicians.

Luckily, it's never been easier to learn the uke than with Guitar Center's free ukulele classes. Every week, we'll present an in-store class designed to teach beginners the basics of the instrument, including tuning, chords and techniques-as well as provide players of all levels the opportunity to play with like-minded musicians.

Miss one? Want a refresher? No problem. The same lesson is presented each week, allowing players to continually hone their newly found ukulele chops.

ThinkAbout: EDUCATE

What is intimidating about the use of your product or service?
How might you create a class about your product?
What would your customers be interested in learning and
how can you position your product as part of that process?
How are you inspiring new customers to try your product?

ou read it in the business press all the time—advice for brands: It's all about content. Think like a publisher. Tell a story. Repurpose. Engage. Interact.

But without authors, publishers would have nothing to publish. I'd like to recommend the following to brand builders and product creators: First, think like an author. Have something meaningful and worthy to say. Say it like no one else. Pour your heart into it. Let yourself be surprised by what you create. Offer your work to the world passionately. Then step back and watch what happens.

One of my favorite authors these days is Ann Voskamp, a self-described farm girl from rural Canada and mother of six. A friend had dared her to start a list of things she was grateful for, and to keep writing until she got to a thousand. She took her friend up on the dare. She scribbled on any little piece of paper she could find. Gifts she already received, like "jam piled high on the toast," "cry of blue jay from high in the spruce" and "wool sweaters." Simple, everyday things. This noticing, this chronicling, changed her life. Voskamp composed her thoughts about all this late at night after the kids went to bed and the farm chores were done. She called it *One Thousand Gifts: A Dare to Live Fully.* It is an intensely personal story, poetically written, all about the transformative, holy aspects of gratitude. She wrote it for herself.

Someone suggested she try to get it published. She tried. It was rejected: "Who cares about a farm girl's spiritual journey?" And then, the right agent connected her with just the right publisher (Zondervan) who gave her story full voice. *One Thousand Gifts* has connected on a deep level with city and country dwellers, women and men, young readers and older ones, spiritual seekers and the faith-filled. People are noticing. It's been on the *New York Times* bestseller list for over 60 weeks. She has been called "the C.S. Lewis of our day."

Voskamp would be surprised to think of her work as a "product," or herself as a "brand," but she has unknowingly created both. All she set out to do was notice. And in that process, noticing became an art form, a new happy discipline. She became a master noticer. Combining her

notice
one thousand gifts

lyrical words with gorgeous photography taken around her home and farm, Voskamp's book and blog has, in turn, invited all of her readers to become master noticers.

Take note: thinking like an author might just get you and your products noticed in bold and unexpected ways!

ThinkAbout: NOTICE

Noticing is all about looking at things through a new lens. Noticing leads to bigger and deeper conversations. Write down three things you notice about your product. Ask a few of your customers to do the same. Ask a few non-customers to do likewise. Study those lists. Take note: what actions will you implement based on this journey of noticing? Try this same exercise all over again with a product outside your industry and then again with one from your competitive field.

On the same day I read the *Wall Street Journal* headline, "Workers Saving Too Little to Retire," I discovered that ING U.S., a retirement, insurance and investment management firm, launched a campaign to help prompt Americans to increase their retirement savings program. They are calling it Orange Money (based on their brand color) and positioning it as the way to accelerate long term savings. Cautioning us to not think of all our green money as spendable—but to think of some of it as Orange Money . . . savable and necessary for retirement.

"The theme of this campaign is more than simply about saving—it's about prioritization, so that you feel like you're in control of your financial future," said Ann Glover, ING U.S. chief marketing officer. "More importantly, the ads show how being prudent with your 'Orange Money' and sensibly managing your personal finances doesn't mean you have to give up living, which you do with your green money."

Through this clever, on-brand multi-media campaign, ING U.S., is providing a practical solution to what the *WSJ* reports is a "retirement crisis—57 percent of U.S. workers surveyed reported less than $25,000 in total household savings and investments excluding their homes." Orange Money is a visual and simple way (much like the old fashioned separate envelope method) for Americans to hasten their savings process.

Here's how this "product" is being promoted on their website:

When you have a clearer idea of the money you can spend now and the money you should save and manage for the future, it makes planning for retirement a whole lot easier.

And that's exactly what we'll help you do. At ING, we have the tools, tips and guidance to help you create a plan for retirement that will make you feel confident about tomorrow while enjoying today.

So, have fun spending spend your green money today. Got Orange Money? ING U.S. is standing by, ready to help you invest it wisely!

prompt

ThinkAbout: PROMPT

Sometimes, a simple picture tells the best story. Like Orange Money, is there a clear visual symbol that would help tell and sell your product story more effectively? Is there some way that your product can prompt your customers to achieve their goals? In today's time pressed world, speed matters. Where might your product development cycle need to be hastened in any way to make you more competitive?

"alk, eat, live, laugh" is the campaign that Yalumba, Australia's oldest family-owned winery is presently promoting. Yalumba, an aboriginal word meaning "all the land around," has been crafting wines for over 160 years. My husband and I had the joy of experiencing Yalumba's winery first hand on our most recent excursion to Australia. For the vintners at Yalumba, wine is all about sharing. Their philosophy: "What you get out of a bottle of wine is just as important as what we put in it."

Because of both our memorable first-hand experience and our enjoyment of their wines, we often serve Yalumba when we are with friends and family. I was thrilled to discover that Yalumba, a brand already a step ahead of its customers, knew that people

would want to share their name and type of wine. They made it convenient with a small label that simply and easily tears off their main label to share with others. A mini-wine business card shall we say! Easier than carrying around the cork! Brilliant. Make your product both an experience that is share-worthy and then make it über-practical to remember and replicate.

The new campaign for Yalumba's signature Y series of wines, plays up the unique zesty, spicy, lively, quirky and quality notes of each varietal. Here's why they want you to "Just add a Y" to your everyday meals:

There's a Y in personality, and vice versa. Variety has a Y too, as does family and history. Yalumba's Y Series is a range of fresh, fruity and lively wines that reflect the 160 year history of Australia's oldest family-owned winery. There's definitely a Y in quality; each varietal consistently provides great value for money and confirms Yalumba's reputation as Australia's finest independent winemaker. But don't take our word for it, Y not find out for yourself?

ThinkAbout: SHARE

What is conversation-worthy about your products? Can you add a feature or reconfigure some aspect of your product packaging to make it easier for your customers to be brand ambassadors and share stories/recommendations about your product?

*l*iving at 8,100 feet on a divide of the Rocky Mountains is simply breathtaking. We think of the deer that come up to our office windows and the fox that scamper through the backyard and the bluebirds that make nests on our back porch as our pets. We plant lots and lots of colorful annuals each May in our mountain desert soil and hope for the best. Luckily, we have a wholesale greenhouse and nine-acre nursery as a "neighbor" (in Colorado, that means in the adjacent five miles!).

Dutch Heritage Gardens is a labor of love for Aaron and Rosie Van Wingerden, an ambitious, 30-something couple who like to get their hands dirty, nurture young seedlings, watch them blossom in the hands of their retail accounts, and then see them brighten people's patios, window boxes, or porches throughout the summer. You'll find their gorgeous-Ros-ie-designed-proprietary hanging baskets and containers selling at places like Costco and King Soopers.

The Van Wingerdens always knew that while their product category may be plants, they were in the *wow* business. In an interview with *GrowerTalks,* Wingerden explains: "We based our entire business model on impulse-buying. My generation is 'do-it-for-me.' They're not going to get their hands dirty. They don't want to dig in the dirt. They want something they can put on their porch and it looks great for the barbeque they're having that weekend. Come home and it's done. They don't have to think about it."

About six years ago, Dutch Heritage Gardens surprised the local community and opened its large greenhouse for a three-day sale directly to the public. It was a gardener's heaven to wander through a kaleidoscope of color made up of acres and acres of plants. When people were not saying "WOW," they often just stood and paused to take in the beautiful spectacle. This event now is a Memorial Day weekend tradition and the wows haven't stopped. Each year they keep adding to the festival-like experience; guitarists are playing, meat is being barbequed, and this season, they're starting a "make your own combo station" as well as a "kid plant station." Van Wingerden said, "We love sharing our greenhouse directly with the public; sometimes this is the only place kids see how plants are nurtured from seed."

Fast forward to chilly December when Dutch Heritage Gardens is filled with acres and acres of red and pink and white and variegated

poinsettias. Once again, the Van Wingerdens surprised and delighted the local community by rolling up their greenhouse doors one wintery weekend and not only offering wholesale prices to their customers, but offering to take family Christmas pictures in the midst of all the poinsettias. Adorable toddlers and families paused to smile in the aisles. More wows. This could have been a scene in *It's a Wonderful Life*.

For the Van Wingerdens, it really isn't about the plants. It's about this sense of awe and wonder and community and giving back and nurturing the wow factor.

ThinkAbout: WOW!

As a product developer, what is it you are truly creating? What is the emotional essence of your product line? How do you wow and surprise and delight your customers? What new ways might you nurture the wow factor in your product line?

*t*racy Amiral, President of Making It Big, Inc., knows that at times the right clothes (comfortable fit and flattering style with the extra attention to detail that elevate an outfit from basic to beautiful) can make all the difference in a person's attitude and confidence. For her customer segment of plus-sized women (starting at size 22+), feeling and looking good in clothes may matter even more. "Our target audience is constantly bombarded by negative societal messages. Our women are navigating through attitudinal minefields and obstacles all the time. We get the most heart wrenching letters about their painful struggle to find work clothes, play clothes, dressy clothes. The retail fashion marketplace continually marginalizes plus-size women and we offer a refuge; a shopping experience and clothing line designed exclusively for plus-size women."

"At MiB, we have positive associations with the word plus. We think being a plus-size is simply a plus! We are in the business of adding MORE to our customer experience . . . more empathy, more selections, more beauty, more service, more smiles." Amiral continues: "We love our customers. Our customers are a diverse group of women—they are business professionals, they are stay at home moms, they are artists, they are volunteers. They are out and about in the world and the clothes they buy from us truly "plus" their wardrobe. They are fashionable, fun, colorful, and practical. We sell no 'fat clothes.'"

Amiral and her team of merchants find joy in "plussing" their customers with these clothes. "Take a look at this Lanai Tunic—we call it 'art you can wear,'" Amiral explains. "Our women love clothes like this, and they deserve to do business with a brand whose main goal is to help them feel beautiful each and every day. We try to add a plus factor to everything we do—from using plus-size models in all our product presentations, to making over 90 percent of our clothing from natural fibers to 'thinking green' in as many ways as possible (for example: we use 100 percent cotton, linen, silk, wool, rayon, and other fine fabrics primarily. We also purposefully use fiber reactive dyes which are fade resistant and less toxic.) At MiB, we're very proud of plus."

plus

ThinkAbout: PLUS

Does your product "plus" your customers' lives?
Are there other creative ways you can "plus" your product
development efforts? What *more* might your customers
appreciate from your brand?

*i*n sunny Florida, Ted Ehrlichman, COO of Suncoast Workforce, and his team dedicate their work days to the art of work advancement, to connecting job seekers with employers and employers with job seekers. They work together with the Economic Development Corporation of Sarasota County, CareerEdge, Bradenton Area Economic Development Corporation, and local leaders in education, private industry, and community-based organizations. It's a job they all take quite seriously. Ehrlichman shares, "We're in the business of helping both parties advance their goals—employers need trained people to contribute to their brands and keep their competitive edge and our job seekers need to accelerate their careers through new opportunities and training or retraining provided by those employers. We spend our days recruiting, training, and retaining, and advancing!

"We all know that finding a job is indeed hard work. Our favorite words are 'I got a job!' We are a bit like career matchmakers. It is truly heartwarming for all of us here at Suncoast Workforce to advance these connections through our various programs. One of these programs, the Workforce Professional Network serves the transitioning professional by providing a support network designed to build on the seekers' strengths and help hone their skills and talents as they focus on re-employment. We just had another success story from a recent professional who was laid off after 16 years. She had to reinvent and rebrand herself but she landed on her feet. She sent me an email thanking me for suggesting the Network Group and was so grateful for everyone's encouragement

advance

en Espanol

SUNCOAST workforce

Connecting Employers with Career Seekers

Become a Fan to Receive Job Alerts

Follow Us to Receive Job Alerts

| Home | Post a Career | Find a Career | Newsroom | Calendar | Resources | Contact |

About SW
Business Services
Career Seekers Services
Military Services
Youth Services
Public Notice

Suncoast Workforce is an excellent resource for our community. They went above and beyond on providing input and knowledge in Training and Development.

Tim Graham, VP of Human Resources,
Tervis Tumbler

Tell Us Your Success Story

Employers
> Search for Candidates
> Post a Careers Opening
> Training Grants
> Research and Statistics

Career Seekers
> Search for a Career
> Post a Resume
> Services
> Let Us Help

Breaking News!
New Satellite Office Now Open! Suncoast Workforce Career Center now at SCTI, 4748 Beneva Rd., Sarasota

Get It Now >>

PLAY

Welcome to Suncoast Workforce...
Where Employers and Job Seekers Connect!

If you're an employer looking to recruit or train talented employees, you've come to the right place. Suncoast Workforce is a non-profit corporation that helps businesses attract the highly skilled workforce they need to stay competitive in today's global economy.

---

to not 'sell herself short.' This is why I say we are in the advancing business—advancing individuals' dreams, advancing their confidence, and advancing employers' growth and success."

The Suncoast Workforce sets its own standards quite high and is ranked as one of the top workforce development programs in the country. Ehrlichman adds, "We don't just believe in advancing to the next level as an important activity for our employers or our job seekers. We believe in it for ourselves. We are continually seeking better ways to connect and engage with our constituents, to improve our internal and external processes, to hone all our brand touchpoints. We are constantly learning and stretching ourselves—advancing is our full time job!"

ThinkAbout: ADVANCE

Can your product be advanced in some small way? How has your competition taken its products to the next level? Have you taken the time to listen to your customers' real needs, or fears, or pain points in order to accelerate your learning curve?

*h*ave you ever been to a gathering of like-minded enthusiasts? Whether they are foodies at a South Beach Food & Wine Festival or film buffs at the Sundance Film Festival or writers at an Iowa Writer's Workshop or Springsteen fans at his rock concert or even Harley riders at Sturgis, the air is full of excitement and passion and lust.

It is no different at a Concours d'Elegance, a gathering of prestigious classic cars, whose owners all compete for "Best of Show" and "Best in Class." The name of the event has 17th-century French aristocratic roots when the affluent paraded their horse-drawn carriages around Paris during the summer. As carriages progressed to cars, these elegant gatherings became all about the automobiles.

The luxuriousness of these multimillion-dollar cars is something to behold. The collectors often house these prized possessions in their garages or even museums, rarely to be seen by the public except at Concours shows. Almost like "rolling artwork," the autos are rarely driven and are often transported to these events, then polished and staged to perfection for the judges. Appearance matters. For them, it is sheer joy to showcase these rare automobiles and discuss them with other *passionistas*. They yearn for that connection and often yearn for their next addition to their collection. The attendees at these events yearn for more too. They may dream about one day owning a special car like these or just yearn for the time period that a particular automobile represents.

Today, Concours d'Elegance events are held around the country in beautiful places throughout the season, such as Pebble Beach, Hilton Head, and Amelia Island, Florida. Patty Dowd Schmitz, Co-Chair and Chief Operating Officer of the Bar-

yearn

rington Concours d'Elegance of Chicago, describes the event a bit like a "royal" wedding weekend. "Between 100 and 200 of the world's finest and most rare vehicles are on display, and the weekend features a charity gala event, welcome parties, road rallies, and more. This year, we will be featuring stunning vehicles from the Mullin Automotive Museum in Oxnard, California, as well as Duesenbergs, Indy Cars, Porsches, Corvettes, Mini Cars, Vincent Motorcycles, and pre- and post-War European and American vehicles, including muscle cars. It is car lover's dream. Enthusiasts never want this weekend to end—they are always yearning for more."

ThinkAbout: YEARN

What would happen if your product lovers gathered in a festival atmosphere? What would they yearn for? How would you provide it for them?

*O*ver the years, our family has been blessed by the truly amazing and life-saving work done by the dedicated medical professionals at the Mayo Clinic. Each time we have had a reason to walk through their doors, we have felt their primary value ring true: "The needs of the patient come first." At the Mayo Clinic we never felt like a number, a case, or a generic patient. We felt like a well-loved family member.

Mayo Clinic's mission is simple but profound: "To inspire hope and contribute to health and well-being by providing the best care to every patient through integrated clinical practice, education and research." Entire books have been written about the best practices of this non-profit. It was hard to focus in on just one aspect of all that they offer that is brand-enhancing. However, in learning about Mayo's Center for Individualized Medicine from Caer Rohrer Vitek, Education Program Manager, I knew I had to share the ground-breaking and hopeful work being done by this project. We all may benefit from this work one day.

"Actually everything the Mayo Clinic does is about a personalized approach to medicine," says Vitek. "But here at the Center for Individualized Medicine we specialize in cases that have eluded all the specialists. Our team translates cutting-edge research into patient care. We call this bench-to-bedside . . . we want to advance the research into a tailored health care protocol for the patient as quickly as possible. Individualizing this research provides hope for patients who often come to feeling hopeless."

Here is how the program is described:

In the Center for Individualized Medicine at Mayo Clinic, physicians and scientists are working together to not only make new discoveries in genomic and clinical science, but also translate these breakthroughs into new ways to predict, diagnose and treat disease.

For patients, individualized health care means better health care. Projects in the Center for Individualized Medicine will lead to increased capabilities for doctors to—for each unique patient—predict and perhaps prevent some diseases, take earlier action when diseases do arise, and choose the most effective medications and treatments while minimizing their side effects.

individualize

By spurring new personalized medicine programs and projects, the Center for Individualized Medicine represents the natural next step in Mayo Clinic's long, successful tradition of providing solutions and hope to each of its patients.

ThinkAbout: INDIVIDUALIZE

What if your brand had a Center for Individualized Product Experiences? How would your thinking change? What would you need to do differently? How are you translating your customers' various needs into differentiated product experiences? What is your brand's version of "bench-to-bedside" product translation?

*t*he Republic of Tea merchants give their customers fair warning: "Rose Petal Black Tea is a limited-edition, seasonal blend. When it's gone, it's gone!" I was given this as a gift one Valentine's Day from a friend who knew of my love of roses, hearts, tea, and all things queenly (it was first named Queen of Hearts tea) and was thrilled she found them all rolled into one blissful product. I actually squealed when I opened the canister the first time. The tea looked like potpourri, tiny real pink rosebuds floating amongst the tea leaves. And, it smelled just like my favorite rose perfume. "Oh my gosh," I thought, "How can I possibly drink this? I just want to inhale it and then sprinkle it around all my rooms!"

But drink it I did and wholeheartedly, no less. I thought it was the best tea I had ever had. I went online to order more. I wanted more for myself. I wanted to send it to all my tea drinking friends. But it was gone. I was out of luck. It was a seasonal tea and as I've learned, "when it's gone, it's gone." I was told I had to wait a whole year. I failed at their mission: "A Sip by Sip Rather Than Gulp by Gulp lifestyle." The folks at The Republic of Tea were going to teach me to savor.

I did have many Rose Tea compatriots. Look at what a few others had to say about this blend:

"I read the other reviews before buying this tea about how relaxing and 'take away' this tea is. It was not until I experienced it myself that I was amazed. The aroma in and of itself is perfect and you don't even have to drink it to start experiencing the pure enjoyment of it. Just opening the lid, all of your senses are taken away. It smells like a fresh bouquet, looks beautiful with the full petal presentation, and then . . . the taste and aroma make you feel relaxed and of royalty. So glad I tried this. I am forever a fan."

"Just looking at this tea in the tin makes me happy—chock full of dainty pink rosebuds and rose petals. You can smell a field of roses with each sip—delicious! I'll definitely order it again next year."

"I ordered this tea for the first time last year, and just had to order it again this year. I've had other rose teas, but this one is the best; the rose flavor

savor

is present (with even some tiny whole buds), but not overpowering. The blend is perfection. The one downside is that it's seasonal and gone after Valentine's Day."

The Republic of Tea savors tea like winemakers savor wine. This isn't their only seasonal blend or even year 'round tea worth savoring. It's just my favorite. Just be warned, if you try one, do so sip by sip.

ThinkAbout: SAVOR

How does your product create anticipation in advance of its enjoyment? Would a limited edition protocol on a few of your products increase its pleasure? How might you encourage your customer to truly savor your product experience?

i remember our ninth grade male teacher always chastening us girls each morning: "NO beautifying yourself in homeroom." He was trying to teach us hair and makeup application etiquette as we rolled our eyes and he scurried us off to the ladies room before classes started. In his own way, he was also probably trying to provoke us to think about something even more important: we were beautiful just as we were. (A long overdue thank you, Mr. Benko!)

The Dove Campaign for Real Beauty has been trying to send the same message for almost a decade. This groundbreaking program run by Unilever has one goal: to provoke a global conversation about the need for a wider definition of beauty. As explained on its website:

> Dove has employed various communications vehicles to challenge beauty stereotypes and invite women to join a discussion about beauty. In 2010, Dove evolved the campaign and launched an unprecedented effort to make beauty a source of confidence, not anxiety, with the Dove Movement for Self-Esteem. Dove has created self-esteem-building, educational programs and activities that encourage, inspire and motivate girls around the world. Dove has reached over 7 million girls so far with these programs, and set a global goal of reaching 15 million girls by 2015.

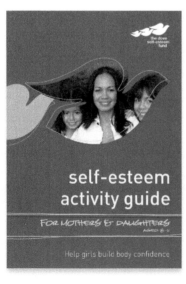

Dr. Nancy Etcoff, Director, Program in Aesthetics and Well Being, Department of Psychiatry, Harvard, kicks off one of Dove's sets of self-esteem boosting activities with this provocative quote: "No young person should leave school feeling that they can't participate fully in life because of the way that they think they look."

What Dove has done has truly given its category a makeover. Instead of selling the soap, the problem, the model perfect face, it is taking a deeper, more strategic and longer view and certainly, aspiring to a higher mission. By awakening young girls' confi-

provoke

☐ flawed?
☐ flawless?

Is beautiful skin only ever spotless? Join the beauty debate.

campaignforrealbeauty.co.uk 🕊 | *Dove*

dence and nurturing self-esteem through this campaign and its global multimedia programs and activities, Dove is beautifying the beauty world. Provoking change. Inside out. Where it really counts.

ThinkAbout: PROVOKE

Might your products be able to be the launch pad to instigate something bigger for your brand? Provoke a deeper conversation or cause or mission? What would it take to makeover your product category in a more meaningful manner? What are you waiting for?

*d*oes the term artful lawyer sound like an oxymoron? In speaking with Miriam DeChant, Esq., Director, Philadelphia Volunteer Lawyers for the Arts, she assures me it is not. "Actually many of the lawyers who volunteer in our program have a true love for the arts. They often pursue some form of the arts as an avocation; they just couldn't have two careers at once! So, thankfully for us (and our artists), they generously volunteer their time to help our clients solve their art-related legal issues."

The Philadelphia Volunteer Lawyers for the Arts (PVLA) is a program offered by the Arts and Business Council of Greater Philadelphia. This council unites business and the arts with the sole purpose of creating connections to make the Greater Philadelphia region culturally vibrant

and economically strong. "It's a win-win-win," says DeChant. "We really believe in the power of uniting these two segments for the greater good of our creative economy. One way we do this is through events—comingling both parties on topics of great interest to both of them. Examples would be guest lectures on topics of creativity, innovation or thought leadership, and presentations on intellectual property issues for the digital environment. This side-by-side learning and sharing unites our business professionals and artists on a more casual basis where real human connections can occur."

DeChant explains further, "Another way we do this is through more typical lawyer-client relationships where an artist may need the expertise and advocacy of one of our pro-bono lawyers. For example, one of our PVLA artful lawyers from DLA Piper, Darius Gambino, united with one of our artists in need, an illustrator who was having legal tangles with the author she collaborated with on a children's book project. Gambino was able to recover her original works, secure her rights, and procure compensation for her from the books that were sold. Our illustrator was

ecstatic. And, Gambino was equally happy. He told us, 'It's the perfect outlet for me. PVLA has allowed me to interact with artists in my hometown and in a way I feel like I have become an artist through my interactions with these people.'

DeChant concludes our conversation this way: "Our community just couldn't be happier about the intertwining of business and arts. We all benefit from this union!"

ThinkAbout: UNITE

Would your product or service benefit from a union with another? What ally with another product/service might create an unexpected win-win-win for your customer? How can a creative partnership enhance your product's potential to add value to your brand?

*i*f you've ever sponsored a child through Compassion International's ministry, then you know their work makes a difference. You know on an emotional level when you receive letters back from your sponsored child talking about their gratitude for the schooling they are receiving, for their books, new shoes, medical care, and extra meals. You just know that your small monthly sponsorship (which adds up to barely a few missed Starbucks or eating in one or two nights instead of getting take out) goes quite far in the oppressed homelands of Guatemala, Ethiopia, El Salvador or any one of the 26 countries Compassion works in. You just know, in your heart and in your head.

But, how often do we take time to validate the work we do? To measure our success ratio? To see if what we thought was working is actually working? To confirm that all our brand energies and product or program development are going towards the right outcomes? Compassion recently had its work validated by independent and empirical research. Results from a University of San Francisco study led by Professor Bruce Wydick and published in the *Journal of Political Economy* found these comparisons between adults who had been sponsored by Compassion as children and their unsponsored peers. They were:

- 50% – 80% more likely to complete a university education,
- about 35% more likely to secure white-collar employment,
- up to 75% more likely to become community leaders as adults,
- and 40% – 70% more likely to become church leaders as adults.

Confirmation that the work Compassion is doing as the "world's leading authority in child sponsorship" is truly making a difference. David Dahlin, Executive Vice President, was not at all surprised by this study: "The children we serve are in desperate need, so effectiveness matters a great deal to us. Although we've witnessed the success of our holistic child development program for decades, we appreciate the external validation of our work. These research results give our sponsors and donors extra confidence in the long-lasting and life-transforming benefits of Compassion's programs, even if they

validate

never take the opportunity to visit the children personally to see our work in action."

A bit about this ministry in case you aren't familiar with them:

Compassion partners with more than 6,000 Christian churches in 26 countries to release more than 1.4 million babies, children and students from poverty. Compassion has the highest rating for financial stewardship and transparency for 12 consecutive years by Charity Navigator, America's largest charity evaluator.

ThinkAbout: VALIDATE

What claims do your products or programs make? How are they validated? How do customers endorse your hard work? What other ways might there be to substantiate your brand promise through your product development efforts?

"What brought you joy as a child?" life coaches and psychologists often ask adults when they are helping them find or rekindle passions later in life. Dylan Lauren, daughter of entrepreneur and brand-builder, Ralph Lauren, already knew her answer: starting at age six, she loved *Willy Wonka & the Chocolate Factory* and the idea of living in a la la candyland. Fast forward to her adult life where that childhood dream became her real life through her creation of Dylan's Candy Bar, an emporium that is even better than anything that Willy Wonka himself could fantasize about.

No doubt inheriting some of her father's creative genius for imagining brands-bigger-than-life, Lauren's mission has been "to merge fashion, art and pop culture with candy to awaken the creative spirit and inner child within all." While candy is at the heart of all Lauren does, it is her magnificent juxtapositioning of merchandise in and around the candy that make this no ordinary confectionery company.

By elevating candy as a platform to create a whole phantasmagoria of sheer delight, Lauren has created an original concept that is colorful and ever-evolving. Here's how she ties together a few categories on her site:

We at Dylan's Candy Bar love candy so much, we want to wear it—and you can too with our candy-inspired tee shirts, tanks, pajamas, hoodies and more. Our candy-colored jewelry and accessories, like our "I Love Candy" bangles (featured in *InStyle*) and Whirly Pop Tote, will add sweet accents to any outfit.

And though we believe candy is the best reward for a hard day's work, sometimes you need to Re-Treat from it all. Enter Dylan's Candy Bar Re-Treat: a collection of spa products inspired by favorite candy flavors, designed to cleanse, soothe and melt stress away.

It's hard to keep up with Lauren—new stores are opening with candy cocktail bars (for those over 21), new license agreements are being inked (for both edible and non-edible product lines), and she's hinted that Dylan's Candy Bar might be expanding into some airports and hotels. The sweet juxtapositioning continues . . .

Here's a playful product that brings joy just by looking at it, let alone eating it, Dylan's Candy Bar Candy-Filled Briefcase:

Your travels won't be complete, without this pre-packed transparent acrylic briefcase! There is something for everyone in this keepsake.

juxtapose

And this is what one customer had to say:

"Recently purchased this for our Dad as a retirement gift . . . thinking it'd be great for him to share with the grandkids . . . but he actually loved it himself! Highly recommended as an executive gift, it really put a smile on his face."

ThinkAbout: JUXTAPOSE

Mix and match and merge and mingle . . . how can you creatively juxtapose some new variables to add more excitement to your merchandise mix? What if you and your team were to spend some time in a la la land fantasy world discussion about your products? How might you build a "lifestyle" around one of your bestselling categories?

i am an Italian girl who grew up eating pizza as my family's soul food. Our dad liked to make us homemade pizza when we would come home from college or just because. Nowadays, we often eat pizza in his memory and honor, and for any and all occasions and, as my sister likes to say, "on days that end in Y."

So, I completely surprised myself by falling for another form of fast nourishment (and from a different ethnicity no less!) when I stumbled upon the wholesome burrito bowl at Chipotle. Steve Ells founded Chipotle with a vision of Food With Integrity. He describes it this way: "Chipotle is seeking better food from using ingredients that are not only fresh, but that, where possible, are sustainably grown and naturally raised with respect for the animals, the land, and the farmers who produce the food."

Ells keeps his product simple: you have a few key choices to make: burritos, tacos, or burrito bowls (minus the tortilla) and then decisions on the fillings: Responsibly Raised® grilled chicken, steak or pork or vegetarian and then all the delightful extras: rice, beans, lettuce, salsas, guacamole, and more. (The folks at Chipotle guesstimate that these seemingly limited choices allow for over 60,000 unique combinations.) You have full view of your food being prepared. You actually don't even mind the long line ahead because it moves ever so quickly (sometimes serving 300 customers per hour) and you know you'll soon be in your own burrito bliss. Chipotle's goal is "to serve food fast so that our customers can enjoy it slowly." Ells' brand is really all about a cycle of nourishment—from his employees to his customers, from his partners and suppliers to his farmers. He says all this nourishing is simply part of doing the responsible thing and "cultivating a burritoful world."

nourish

MENU OUR MENU ISN'T LONG – BUT IT'S LONG ON OPTIONS. START WITH THE BASICS AND CUSTOMIZE AS NEEDED TO BUILD YOUR PERFECT MEAL.

BURRITO   BURRITO BOWL   CRISPY TACOS   SOFT TACOS   SALAD   CHIPS & GUAC   KID'S MENU

Ingredients

Fresh Cooking

Nutrition
Calculator

Special Diet
Information

Ingredients
Statement

I'M NOT ADDICTED

I JUST EAT 'EM EVERY DAY

Burrito
Flour tortilla, choice of cilantro-lime rice, pinto or vegetarian black beans, meat (braised carnitas or barbacoa, adobo-marinated and grilled chicken or steak) or guacamole, salsa and cheese or sour cream.

Chipotle recently decided to upsize its nourishment factor and created an entire catering program for groups of 20 to 200 by allowing them to customize their own individual meal just like they do at a restaurant. Says Ells: "With catering, we can now better serve our customers by allowing them to bring Chipotle into their homes, office and schools where they conveniently and effortlessly share the food they love with large groups of people." His loyal brand fans say bring on the extra nourishment!

ThinkAbout: NOURISH

How does your product feed your customer's soul?
What aspect is most life-giving? What aspect might be
upsized to create a bigger impact? As a product creator,
how are you nourishing your own creative soul?
Where might you need or find extra nourishment?

i had a short but profound conversation with Mike Faith, CEO and President of Headsets.com about his customers, his brand, and his headsets. "It's simple, for us, it all comes down to love. We've built a brand around loving our customers, treating them with respect and really caring about winning them over. We love our headsets and we love matching the right product to the right customer."

I asked Faith which headset he loved the best. He didn't hesitate. "It's easy; it's the Sennheiser Wireless OfficeRunner. We co-branded this with our vendor and our goal was to develop a headset with all the specs we knew our customers would love: best range, lightest weight, best warranty, appealing design. This headset really hits it out of the park."

IER Partners is a Headsets.com customer. Faith is right. Not just about this headset, but about his whole business philosophy. Look at a few reviews for this model and see how often the word love shows up:

> "This is the third headset I've bought this year! I got one for myself first and now I've gotten one for both of my assistants. We *love* everything about them, especially the ability to run the computer sound into the headset. This is a fast-paced environment where mistakes can destroy us. The extra efficiency and comfort we've gained have been great."

> "I *love* it. Everyone in my office has tested mine and wants one now, too. I'm ordering two more now and possibly more later! It works great working between the computer and the phone and that's exactly what I needed. The rest of the office staff enjoys the light weight and the clarity."

> "*Love* the OfficeRunner. Very comfortable. Works great with my phone system, easier to install than Plantronics. Great sound quality, did not have to adjust a thing. Magnetic base works great. *Love* it!"

By the way, Faith and his team put a little extra love in all outgoing orders. Each package has a heart sticker on it which contains the words, "Packed with Customer Love by _____" and includes the name of the person who packed it. Once opened, the customer will find a couple

love

Tootsie Rolls, yet another way to convey the company's fondness for their customers and appreciation for their business!

ThinkAbout: LOVE

What aspects of your products are beloved by your customers?
How can you infiltrate more love into all you do—
co-developing products with your partners, serving your
customers, winning their long-term, repeat-purchase affection?

i was first introduced to ZÜCA when I met my friend, Joani Schultz, Chief Creative Officer, GROUP Publishing, at The Brown Palace in Denver for a girls' getaway weekend earlier this year. She was *sitting* on it in the lobby waiting for me to arrive. Adjusting to some walking issues related to a health condition and needing to sit more than stand these days, my always optimistic, world-travelling, business-owning friend said, "I couldn't survive without my ZÜCA." Exact quote. "This ZÜCA goes with me everywhere."

Catch a few more Z's

Considerate design is used in all ZÜCA accessories! We've got stuff to protect your buns, your back and your bag. We can help keep your ride rolling smooth and always unique, and if there is an accessory you would like to see, be sure to let us know!

Shop Now!

I smiled then when I was on a plane later that month and saw the headline of the latest ZÜCA ad in *Fortune* magazine: "Only the strong survive." Bruce Kinnee, President of ZÜCA, Inc., says, "The ZÜCA Flyer was specifically designed for hard-core business travelers. From the ultra-durable fabric to the chrome accents and weight platform, to customized compartments for tablets, ear buds, smartphones and more, we have weaved in the most sought-after features every business traveler wants." The ad goes on to explain the key "beauty and brawn" features of The Flyer. It is fully FAA compliant, slides easily down tight plane aisles and is compact enough to fit in overhead bins, and holds up to 300 lbs. It's a suitcase that not only outperforms other suitcases in a traditionally competitive way; it outmaneuvers the entire category by adding a whole new component—a seat!

ZÜCA Founder, Laura Udall, an innovative mother of three, first created ZÜCA in response to back problems her children were incurring by lugging the heavy backpacks that had become the school norm. She wanted a product that would not only solve the carrying issues her children faced in a "cool" way, but one that would outperform all other

outperform

models in terms of durability, health, and safety. Her surprise in the early years of the company was that the response from adults outperformed even the children! They all wanted their own ZÜCA! Today, the team at ZÜCA continues to outperform its competitors and prides itself on "developing super-durable, absurdly versatile travel carry-alls for the fast pace world of today's consumer looking for lasting quality."

ThinkAbout: OUTPERFORM

Is there one aspect of your product that outmaneuvers all
others in your category? Is it conversation-worthy?
How have you promoted it? What are your plans
to continue this outperforming behavior?
Do you have any "brawn and beauty" comingling in your line?

*i*s there anything more exuberant and life-giving than being around young girls, full of laughter and energy and movement? Seeing girls jump for joy, dance enthusiastically and run with all they've got for just the sheer pleasure of it all makes you want to stop what you're doing and join them right then and there! The brand developers and merchants at lululemon, a yoga-inspired athletic company for women, turned their merchandising attention to "active girls who love to move and aren't afraid to sweat" and created ivivia. Here's how they describe it:

> ivivva athletica was created based on extensive feedback from lululemon guests who wanted dance specific products for a younger age group using similar signature fabrics, technical design features and exciting colors for which lululemon is known. ivivva products are designed for athletic pursuits such as dance and gymnastics, as well as for all-day versatility.

lululemon's inspirational manifesto doesn't include the verb vivify but it certainly permeates all their product actions and launches . . . their clothes help give life to their customers' passion for movement, whether that is dance or yoga or running . . . and whether those females are 8 or 48.

ivivia speaks the language of its youthful target audience complete with lots of exclamation marks and things like a "Tanks Quiz" and "bff notes" and product copy about why each clothing item "rocks." Here is what they have to say about their anything-but-routine Routine Jacket:

- Warm up like a superstar in this multi-sport jacket
- luon® fabric has a cotton-feel and 4-way stretch to move with you
- Zipper pockets for your cash, keys, and phone
- Thumbholes help keep sleeves down and palms warm

And, what a young figure skater had to say:

> "It keeps me so warm on the ice especially on the days I skate for 2-3 hours. I don't get as cold. Very easy to layer under things. I got this jacket in the lavender. Mine fits perfectly and still has some growing room. I really want another color for my birthday!! Thanks ivivva!!"

Another key to ivivia's success is that they purposefully involve their target audience in all they do. (This is part of lululemon's brand DNA as well.) With a "Help Us Design" tab on their site, they remind girls that it is *their* input that gives life to ivivia's merchandise and always invites feedback for ways they can improve their products:

> ivivva makes dancewear and active wear for girls that is designed with input from you! We talk to gymnasts, dancers, and athletes in our communities every day to find out what works, what doesn't, and what you'd love to wear Thanks for help making our stuff rock!

These young girls are seriously passionate about this brand. They don't want to outgrow ivivia. Presently, ivivia's sizes stop at 14 and the girls are clamoring for them to make size 16. More life! More life!

ThinkAbout: VIVIFY

What is life-giving about your product line? Do you have customers clamoring for more of what you do? What feedback system is in place for your customers to add more life/input/ feedback into your product development process?

"Clothing that comforts. That's what we do," Jan Erickson, Founder and President of Janska, a women's clothing manufacturer, recently explained to me. "It started with just a simple dream; I wanted to help people live more comfortably and easily—and in style. Years ago, I was visiting a woman in a nursing home and I noticed she would sometimes have her coat on backward because that was the only way her care attendants would be able to slip it on her; or worse, she was lying there, freezing cold, in one of those horrid hospital gowns. It was painful to see. I wanted her to have some warmth and dignity. So I had a jacket, with a slit up the back and large loose fitting sleeves, specially made for her. When I slipped the fleece jacket over her head, she smiled and exhaled."

"Then, all these other ideas just started tumbling into my head," Erickson said. "Janska was born. I firmly believe clothes shouldn't add stress to your life. All of our clothes provide comfort in some way."

Practically every product in her line feels like your very own adult blankie, and from what her customers say, these clothes also soothe and calm like blankies, too! One of her earliest products, the patented, perennially-bestselling, LapWrap®, can be worn out and about like a short cape or pulled around you while watching your favorite episode of Downton Abbey. Here's how Erickson describes it:

> The original wrap that started it all—two garments in one! Use it as a shawl over the shoulders for the perfect fit and just a bit of extra warmth. Or as a lap blanket—handsomely contoured shape covers the legs, but doesn't drag the ground. Clean, flowing lines. Lightweight, soft, and warm. Unique toggle button closure. Perfect for home or traveling! Made in the USA of washable Polartec® fleece. One size fits most.

Comfort is clearly Erickson's product filter. But so is looking good. She's not willing to compromise comfort for style. "Every garment we create must pass our consummate test: 'Do I love wearing this?'" Her customers include travelers, hard-to-buy-for elderly, or women of all ages who want to look fashionable while keeping warm in their homes or offices.

comfort

ThinkAbout: COMFORT

What product kicked off your company's early success?
Is there some aspect of that product that soothes your
customers in some way? Does your product bring your
customers more comfort than your competitors?
Why or why not? Is there anything stressful about using
your products that you might need to attend to?

*m*akeup artist and entrepreneur, Bobbi Brown, just plain gets women. Her motivation "has always been to help women be confident and feel comfortable being themselves." Based on this, she launched an initiative called Pretty Powerful Campaign for Women & Girls. In her words, "I think all women are pretty, and with the right tools, are empowered to a higher level of pretty. This campaign began as a message about the power of beauty but is now a full-fledged global initiative to empower women and girls around the world with the confidence and resources to be their best."

Bobbi Brown's career and the eponymous brand she built has been all about transporting women—captivating and elevating them to be their best selves. There is one product in her line though that transports women in a slightly different way, right to the sensory experience of having your toes in the sand, on the beach. It's her perfume called simply, BEACH. Here is what her delighted customers have to say:

"This fragrance smells like heaven in a bottle! If you love the smell of Coppertone, which I do, you will love this. I am totally hooked and I want to smell like this for the rest of my life!"

"Beach is my favorite Summer Fragrance and definite GO TO for an instant vacation day! I am . . . Beach HAPPY! xoxo, a former lifeguard"

"I love its clean scent that reminds me of the sunscreen of my youth. Be prepared for when you wear it that people will comment about how it smells like sunblock in the room, not that it's a bad thing, but you can see the puzzled looks on their faces when they're trying to figure out why it smells like sunblock in January . . . in Michigan. I am a "Beach" devotee!"

"When you use this product, you feel like you are on the beach of some fabulous island. When we can't be on vacation this perfume still makes us feel as if we are."

"I ordered the fragrance having never smelled it and fell in love with it at first whiff. I felt transported to a beautiful white sandy beach. I work with a country band and was wearing Beach. The lead singer came up to me with her eyes wide and said, "What are you wearing you smell like a beach?" What more can be said? I love this fragrance!!!!"

transport

I could add my own enthusiastic testimonial to these. While I love living in the Rocky Mountains, I am a beach girl at heart. This perfume evokes nothing but blissful island experiences and transports me with every spray. Pretty powerful in its own right!

ThinkAbout: TRANSPORT

What sensory associations might your products evoke?
Are your customers transported in some positive way through
your product experiences? How can you evoke even more
powerful connotations through your creations?

i wonder how many merchants and product creators consider themselves "soul makers"?

The brand-builders at Montblanc do and proudly state: "Soul-Makers for 100 Years. In days gone by, people believed that if a person touched an object, that object would form a bond with a part of their soul. Today such a thought seems almost absurd . . . Until you enter the realm of Montblanc's master craftsmen."

I wonder how many merchants and product creators "hold their breath in order to create a perfect product?"

The watchmakers at Montblanc do and proudly state: "Watch over your precious moments mindfully. At Montblanc, our master craftsmen hold their breath in order to create perfect timepieces. The smallest exhalation could disrupt the delicate system of crafting a timepiece by hand. We delightfully hold our breaths so that you don't have to." At right is one breathtaking example of a timepiece from Montblanc's Profile line.

Upholding the heritage of this luxury brand is a job everyone at Montblanc takes seriously. As a matter of fact, it's part of their brand philosophy:

In today's ever-increasing pace, it is paramount to be confronted with products that have been crafted to withstand the passing of time. Montblanc's pieces will weather the ages with you and witness the unfolding stories of you and your family. Just as a soul remains long after a body is gone, our pieces are crafted to perform superbly and brandish elegance for many lifetimes.

In the luxury market, Montblanc's reputation is about as high as the real Mont Blanc in the Alps. They value their reputation dearly and know their customers do too. They do not take it for granted even after 100+ years of luxury craftsmanship, but rather want to insure its future legacy. To uphold their watchmaking heritage, they've founded the Institute of Swiss Watchmaking to insure that there will always be "dedicated, career-minded individuals with the education and training excellence."

Pam Danziger, President of Unity Marketing and author of *Putting the Luxe Back in Luxury,* shares her thoughts on the importance of upholding heritage for a luxury marketer such as Montblanc: "There are no 'instant' luxury brands. It takes time, sometimes decades, often a century, to build a heritage that entitles a company to claim the 'luxury brand'

uphold

MONT BLANC

title. A brand like Montblanc started with a single extraordinary idea—create the ultimate writing instruments that deliver the ultimate writing experience. But it took many years to translate the brand into a symbol that communicates the user's appreciation of that ultimate luxury writing experience. From that place of strength, Montblanc was able to extend their product line into new categories like watches."

ThinkAbout: UPHOLD

Whether your brand is 100 months or 100 years old, it has a legacy. What is yours? How are your products purposefully upholding that legacy? What specific product attributes are connected to your brand legacy? Are they breathtaking?

*S*ome people just do not understand why you would watch someone cook. Brooke Johnson, President of The Food Network, explains it this way: "Twenty years ago experts would never have predicted the passion our little network would stir up. Food allows people to explore, experience and connect with the world around them." Johnson knows what she is talking about: The Food Network is being watched by more than 100 million households and its success led to the launch of a second network, Cooking Channel. It has invited chefs like the Barefoot Contessa (Ina Garten), Rachel Ray, Mario Batali, Jamie Oliver, Bobby Flay, and many more into America's kitchens and motivated its viewers to be doers not just watchers. With its own magazine, on-line store, recipe sharing, contests and blog, The Food Network prompts its viewers to find their own way in the kitchen.

Known by just her first name, Giada de Laurentis, one of The Food Network's celebrity female chefs, began her show in 2002. It's fair to say she motivates while she marinates! She exudes enthusiasm and conveys a real love for her audience. She wants you to try these recipes at home, add your own twist and most of all, try and enjoy! She introduces you to her aunt, her husband, and her daughter in daily life situations so you get to know her as a person, not just a personality. She's the "cook next door" and her love of family, recipes, and gathering people together shines through.

Motivating ancillary products like her namesake food items (such as Giada Marinara Sauce with Artichokes) and branded cookware (both available at Target), easy to follow cookbooks (*Everyday Pasta*, *Weeknight Dinners*) and cooking at live events like the SOBE Wine and Food Festival in Miami, connects Giada with her viewers in ways that inspire them to put her recipes on their tables.

Here's what she writes in her latest cookbook:

"This is what weeknights look like in my house. I hope these recipes inspire you and your family to gather around the table (or picnic blanket!) for some fantastic dinners—and, most important, a whole lot of fun. Buon appetite!"—Giada

How do you say "very motivating!" in Italian?

motivate

weeknights with Giada

Giada De Laurentiis

quick and simple recipes to revamp dinner

ThinkAbout: MOTIVATE

Do your products turn your customers into doers?
What additional prompts might they need to fully experience
the depth of your brand? Using The Food Network as a model,
how can you, as a product developer, repurpose more of your
product's best features across channels, product lines and
partnerships to motivate your customers to reach their goals?

*d*ave & Debbie Hammer of Hammer Homes guarantee it: "We build your home as if it were our own!" With over 30 years of custom construction experience, the Hammers know just how personal it is to build someone's home. They also know that overdelivering is the way to grow your business. Here's what they have to say: "Our success has been directly attributed to detail, communication, quality workmanship, competitive pricing and the strong commitment we have to our clients. We stand behind our product 100 percent."

One of the things that sets Hammer Homes apart is their specialty in building ADA Accessible homes. Dave Hammer knows about these needs firsthand as he has lived in a wheelchair since an accident that occurred in 1987. The Hammers have branded these "The Forever Home" Collection, and describe them this way:

> We woke up one morning and were empty nesters. That started the Cottage Collection. We didn't need all that space any more, but we wanted the nice finishes and main level living. We designed the ranchers with main level everything, but a lovely lower level for family, grandchildren or guests. Then, four years later, we realize we baby boomers are retiring at 10,000 a day. Where are we all going to live? The Forever Home was born. Now you can live in a home that you will be able to stay in forever. Our Forever Homes are completely accessible for you and your loved ones future needs . . . complete with wider doors, hallways, no step entrys, roll in showers, elevators and much more. Until you have lived with needs, you really have no idea what you will need. Why not have a home you will be able to stay in? We even have complete lower level private living for family or nurses' quarters.

Michael Brennan of Hammer Homes knows about the importance of overdelivering. "Building a home is personal, it's a special place, and we get that. We are building YOUR house. It just doesn't get any better than that! We tell our clients, 'You don't have to go on vacation to enjoy resort style living. You can have it right here at home.' We meet with our clients weekly while their homes are under construction. Building a home can be very stressful and our clients have lots of questions throughout the process. We want our clients to be thrilled with their new home. We overcommunicate. Contractors often don't do that. Coupled with

overdeliver

our integrated co-construct software program, our clients know all the details and timetables of their project. They are involved every step of the way. They appreciate our expertise, creativity and exacting standards. For me, at the end of the day, it comes down to trust and relationships. These values are deeply rooted in our company. Honestly, overdelivering is our norm."

ThinkAbout: OVERDELIVER

As a product developer, do any of your creations stem from personal experience? How have you leveraged this in your brand building? Compared with others in your industry, are your products under or overdelivering? What one detail of your product line might benefit from some turbocharging?

*d*o you ever wonder how many bucket list items never get checked off? How many life dreams are deferred? How many creative pursuits are left undone? How many projects stay scribbled on cocktail napkins? How many ideas remain just that?

What if all that could change by simply hitting some "ACTIVATE" button on your computer? A button that nudges you towards your goals, a button that invites friends and strangers to weigh in on your dreams and help make them happen through participative funding? A button that boosts your morale and gives you the confidence to make your mark on the world and cheer you along? What if it were simply that easy to kick start those dreams, creative pursuits, and projects?

Well, enter Kickstarter.com. Here's how they explain it: "Thousands of creative projects are funding on Kickstarter at any given moment. Each project is independently created and crafted by the person behind it. The filmmakers, musicians, artists, and designers you see on Kickstarter have complete control and responsibility over their projects. They spend weeks building their project pages, shooting their videos, and brainstorming what rewards to offer backers. When they're ready, creators launch their project and share it with their community. Every project creator sets their project's funding goal and deadline. If people like the project, they can pledge money to make it happen. If the project succeeds in reaching its funding goal, all backers' credit cards are charged when time expires. If the project falls short, no  one is charged. Funding on Kickstarter is all-or-nothing."

Like those donors receiving free tote bags on PBS, activating backers on Kickstarter do indeed receive rewards in return for their pledges to projects (Two examples: pledge $10 receive a DVD of the film, pledge $5,000 have dinner with creators).

Granted, it does take a bit more than hitting just one button, but Kickstarter activates both products and projects. Emily Reese of Kickstarter's Community Team spoke about the power of this activation: "Every day Kickstarter is part of the birth process of making people's dreams come

activate

true. It's inspiring to be part of that process. We participate in the whole cycle of innovation—from helping get the word out about these dreams to uniting backers around these dreams to seeing the dreamers reap the satisfaction of their dreams being realized."

ThinkAbout: ACTIVATE

Is there an aspect of your product that helps activate a deep-seated dream of your customers? How can you play up this important role in your product development? Are you involved in the whole cycle of innovation with your product line?

*b*efore we go too far in talking about these adorable marshmallow candies, take a peek at these Peeps® Fun Facts from its company's website, Just Born:

- Just Born got its name when founder, Sam Born, proudly displayed in his store window an evolving line of daily-made candy, declaring them "just born."

- In 1953, it took 27 hours to create one Peeps Marshmallow Chick. Today, thanks to advances in technology, it takes six minutes.

- Just Born produces enough Peeps® Brand Marshmallow Candies in one year to circle the earth twice.

- In the late 1950s Peeps wings were "clipped" to give them a sleek, modern look.

- Peeps Brand Candies have been the #1 non-chocolate brand confection at Easter for over 20 years. *(Source: IRI Total U.S. FDMx)*

- Yellow is America's best-selling color of Peeps chicks and bunnies.

- Peeps have become gourmet favorites in fondues, as a crème brûlée ingredient, and as cappuccino toppings!

Everyone probably has a childhood Peeps story as part of their Easter celebrations. But now, as the company has grown and seasonalized those Peeps, those stories can encompass many other holidays. No longer just available at Easter, Peeps in one form or another can be part of your Valentine's Day, Halloween, Christmas, and even year round. Just Born has taken full creative advantage of the opportunities the calendar presents with surprises and shapes and flavors like Chocolate Mousse Flavored Marshmallow Reindeer to Vanilla Crème Flavored Marshmallow Hearts.

seasonalize

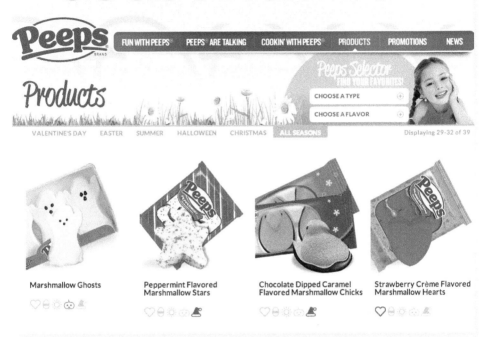

| Marshmallow Ghosts | Peppermint Flavored Marshmallow Stars | Chocolate Dipped Caramel Flavored Marshmallow Chicks | Strawberry Crème Flavored Marshmallow Hearts |

However, these clever whimsical candies are just the back drop for much more brand seasonalizing. Just Born partnered with Volkswagen Beetle and has its own *Peepster* vehicle that creates brand awareness around the country at various events and shares Random Acts of Sweetness. In addition, its website encourages all sorts of ways for customers to express their *Peepsonality* through entertaining pins, recipes, and photos.

What impressed me most was the last line in their brand philosophy: We believe our work has just begun.

ThinkAbout: SEASONALIZE

What holiday best represents your brand?
Can the successes from that season be a springboard for others? What whimsical ways might you surprise and delight your customers through seasonal product promotions?
What is waiting to be "just born" in your product offering?

*a*ngie Schwab loves where she lives and works so much she has made a career out of promoting it. As the Community and Economic Development Specialist for the County of Humboldt, California, Schwab sings the area's praises: "Our clean air and ocean breezes and rugged redwoods and simple living lure people here. The people here in Humboldt County appreciate our rural sophistication and have designed purposeful, happy, healthy lives. We love our direct access to grass-fed beef, lamb, poultry as well as oysters and crab. We grow our own cheese, flowers, organic foods. We make our own beer, wine, chocolates. But it isn't easy living. We are truly a community of bootstrappers. We do not have all the resources or conveniences of a big city like San Francisco. But this is also what makes us strong: our sense of community and like-mindedness towards entrepreneurialism, innovation, inventiveness and perseverance. As Don Banducci, one of our board members, says, we're 'comrades in farms'!"

Humboldt is the home for an eclectic assortment of businesses, ranging from breweries to musical instruments to organic and specialty foods to flowers and jewelry designers and manufacturers. To name just a few: Mad River Brewing, Eel River Organic Beef, Marimba One, Baroni Designs, Riverbend Cellars, Humboldt Cheese and Dairy, Humboldt Hot Sauce and the Sun Valley Group. These innovators and entrepreneurs have bootstrapped their way to successful businesses and now have banded together to promote the region with Schwab's help.

Economic Development launched Humboldt Made in order to promote this area more fully and help it gain further recognition. It's a consortium of local businesses that are proud to be a part of Humboldt and have authentic products to offer the whole nation. Schwab believes, "Branding the regional qualities of Humboldt County is an ideal way for our product developers and producers to differentiate their products in a crowded, global marketplace. Promoting 'Humboldt Made' makes each member of the consortium a brand ambassador for this area and strengthens our impact."

promote

Photo courtesy of Vorce Construction.

ThinkAbout: PROMOTE

Many companies "bake" their promotional efforts right into their product development efforts. How might you turn up the volume on promoting your products? Is there potential strength in combining efforts in some creative way?

When did bootstrapping advance your product development efforts? How did those limitations launch creativity? Why might "forced bootstrapping" be a good part of risk-taking?

*f*resh Produce wants dressing to be a piece of cake, or, perhaps, like picking out a piece of colorful fresh produce—uncomplicated, enjoyable, and easy. For the last three decades, Mary Ellen and Thom Vernon have built their clothing company, Fresh Produce, with one vision in mind: keep it all simple. The Vernons' stated goal is "to inspire women to live life and enjoy color." They accomplish this through a collection of seasonless skirts, tops, bottoms, and dresses in vibrant prints and colors that feature a signature garment dye process. Their line retails entirely under $100 and is primarily made in the USA. Their clothes make you smile.

The smart merchants at Fresh Produce encourage their customers to live the "FP Life." Here is how they explain it:

> The heart of Fresh Produce is rooted in the positive impact of color. We love color and want our customers to light up the room in our clothes. From casual tops and feminine dresses to decorative scarves and stylish pants, Fresh Produce is dedicated to creating feel-good clothes women want to wear every day. The coastal-inspired colors and broad assortment of easy-to-wear pieces are flattering and comfortable on all shapes and sizes and are available in Extra Fresh plus sizes as well as children's styles. The comfortable fabrics, fit and style reflect carefree ease.

NEW
COLORS
TO LOVE »

I first encountered Fresh Produce clothing while browsing a seaside store on vacation and immediately wished that my whole wardrobe was like this—soft, effortless clothes that evoke beach and lake and boardwalk memories. Easy, uncomplicated living. The splashes of turquoise, pink, coral, and bright green mixed with the prints of seashells, flip flops, and starfish all launched the company.

Melanie Hohag, a longtime Fresh Produce fan, says it best: "It's as simple as this: Fresh Produce = summer! Whether I spot a new item in

uncomplicate

the store or pull last year's shirt out of my drawer, the bright colors and effortless fit say 'go have a great day in the sun!'"

While these "beach clothes" are still a significant part of the line, the merchants have transposed this uncomplicated vibe into year-round clothes that fit the same criteria: carefree ease.

ThinkAbout: UNCOMPLICATE

Is uncomplicating your customers' lives part of your product development process? If not, should it be? Do your products make your customers smile? Do they "light up a room" in some way? Does color play a part of your sensory product experience? How can you uncomplicate one aspect of getting your product to market?

i have always loved typography. The playfulness of lettering and ink paying homage to each important letter of the alphabet. I loved how each letter seemed to have its own unique personality and boldness of character. Wouldn't you agree that the letter A projects an entirely different persona from the letter K and from an X? So, I was thrilled to discover that the masterly merchants at Williams Sonoma decided to create a new line of products specifically marked with the flourish of type and design. Named Mark and Graham, this is how they describe their new launch:

> We believe that a mark is more than a symbol;
> It's an artful mingling of typography and design
> that turns a gift into a personal gesture.
> It can be bold and boisterous
> or subtle and refined.
> It can join families together
> or celebrate individuality.
> It can be an inside joke
> or honor the literal beauty
> of a name.

In a company release about the launch, Marta Benson, Senior Vice President of Strategy and Business Development for Williams-Sonoma, Inc. said, "For a brand to resonate with people, it has to have meaning and a sense of purpose. At Mark and Graham our mission is to help you celebrate the people in your life and to make gift giving personable and fun. The name 'Mark and Graham' is a play on words about creating one's own mark or monogram. We want to share our passion for typography and design, and give customers the tools to create beautiful gifts."

Mark and Graham offers its customers a lovely line of gift items with the added flourish of contemporary fonts and monograms that heighten and personalize the gift-giving experience. The merchants and product creators at Mark and Graham believe this flourish is what "turns a gift into a modern-day heirloom." Whether a customer is "making their mark" on linens or jewelry or gifts for the home or office, this product line presents all sorts of flourish opportunities via 50+ custom monograms

flourish

and options in embroidery, laser-engraving, sandblasting, pad printing, or engraving. This Linen Wine Bag with Grosgrain Tie, for example, can be personalized with a message (Love, Cheers, Congrats!) or a specific monogram.

ThinkAbout: FLOURISH

How can you add flourish to your product line? What masterly sparkle might add even more meaning to your offer?

ears ago this *New York Times* headline caught my attention, "Colleges Offering Campuses as Final Resting Place." It reported, "In an era when many people are highly mobile and do not settle in one place for long, a college can have a strong allure as a final resting place . . . colleges have special resonance for many people, who have forged life-long relationships as undergraduates." The article quoted Rev. David D Burhans, a retired University of Richmond chaplain who helped create its large campus columbarium: "Many people don't identify with their churches or their churches don't have cemeteries like they used to. But people feel very connected to their colleges and there are some beautiful places on campuses."

I thought about loyalty programs and how this really seemed to be the ultimate way to eternalize your brand. A final brand good-bye. A way to memorialize your experience. Then my sister told me that she and her husband had just purchased companion crypts at his alma mater, Notre Dame. The Cedar Grove Cemetery on campus recently opened its burial options to Notre Dame alumni in a program called Coming Home (previously it was open only to Notre Dame faculty and staff).

Father Bill Seetch explains it this way: "We call this new project *Coming Home,* for that is the pervasive feeling found throughout the Notre Dame family. 'It feels like home to me, Father.' I hear that from first year students as well as from graduates out fifty years and more."

Rev. Edward A. Malloy, C.S.C., President Emeritus of Notre Dame said this: "For those nurtured on its campus and proud of its traditions and spirit, Notre Dame evokes a sense of family. Whatever one's origins or time of matriculation or employment, there is a bond that links the generations and makes them comfortable with the symbols, sites and songs of the place."

The Cedar Grove Cemetery truly is a sacred space in a sacred place. My brother-in-law, John Hearn, attorney and Notre Dame alumnus,

eternalize

shares this: "Notre Dame is all about faith and a genuine commitment to excellence and each other. Notre Dame prepares and inspires men and women to contribute meaningfully to the world in many varied ways held together by a commitment to ethics and faith. This small school in northern Indiana was built by poor Catholic immigrants against all odds and prejudices to become one of the most powerful means for good in this country. It is often said, when trying to explain the spirit of Notre Dame that, if you have been to Notre Dame, no explanation is necessary. If you've *not* been to Notre Dame, no explanation will suffice. Being part of that spirit is fully realized by spending all eternity on a campus whose mission is to achieve such an ambitious goal. This is home for us."

ThinkAbout: ETERNALIZE

What memory does your product evoke?
Does your product have a positive lingering effect on your
customers? Is there a way to create a
more lasting impression with your product?

Zondervan, part of HarperCollins Christian Publishing, is a world leading Bible publisher and provider of Christian communications. Their children's division, Zonderkidz, is in the ministry of creating products that teach and inspire children to learn and live out their faith. Annette Bourland, Sr. Vice President & Group Publisher, Zondervan, reminds us that teaching is not preaching. "We take a very

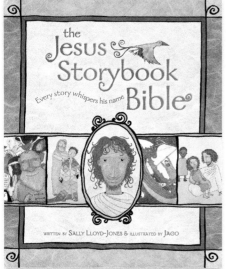

different approach with our products," says Bourland. "Take our Jesus Storybook Bible for example. We knew our storytelling approach wholeheartedly engaged children from 4 to 8 years of age. What we were surprised to discover was that this book became a teaching tool in *adult* markets . . . with seminary professors, in women's ministries, and even in prison ministries. We loved how creatively our author, Sally Lloyd-Jones, was able to teach the Jesus story so effectively to such a broad spectrum of readers."

Here's how Zonderkidz describes this story:

Written for children ages four and up, *The Jesus Storybook Bible* tells the one story underneath all the stories of the Bible and points to the birth of a child, the Rescuer, Jesus. Complete with 44 Bible stories, *The Jesus Storybook Bible* paints a beautiful portrait of Jesus and invites children to see that he is not only at the center of God's great story of redemption—he is at the center of their story too. Children and adults alike will be captivated by the beautifully written narrative and the original and unique illustrations by accomplished artist Jago. Sally Lloyd-Jones' powerful gift of storytelling draws the reader into the greatest adventure of all time in an exciting page-turner that kids (and adults) find hard to put down.

The Jesus Storybook Bible has received multiple awards, including the Moonbeam Award Gold Medal Winner in the religion category. *Christianity Today* has hailed this product as "a very grown up Children's

teach

The Story and The Song
Introduction from Psalm 19 and Hebrews 1

The Heavens are singing
about how great God is;
and the skies are shouting it out,
"See what God has made!"
Day after day... Night after night...
They are speaking to us.

Psalm 19:1-2 (paraphrase)

God wrote, "I love you" — he wrote it in the sky, and
on the earth, and under the sea. He wrote his message
everywhere! Because God created everything in his
world to reflect him like a mirror — to show us what he is
like, to help us know him, to make our hearts sing.
   The way a kitten chases her tail. The way red poppies
grow wild. The way a dolphin swims.
   And God put it into words, too, and wrote it in a book
called "the Bible."

Bible and "as theological as it is charming." Lloyd-Jones elaborates on the power of teaching through this story-telling process: "When I was writing this, I imagined a mother speaking to her children. I wanted to continually point to Jesus and share that the Bible is the most wonderful story. It's a love story where every story is about how much God loves us and has come to rescue us."

This is what Zonderkidz is all about and why they take their mission of teaching, not preaching, so seriously.

ThinkAbout: TEACH

Behind every story is another story. Merchants, editors and product developers create products to tell stories that support their brand promises. What are your products teaching your customers about your brand? What story layers may have yet to be written for your product? Have your customers taught you additional uses for your product? Can your stories be taught in new and unusual ways?

*L*aura Brady, CEO of MPI (Medical Positioning, Inc.) thinks about the verb *position* all the time. Her brand is built around it and it's right there in the company's name. MPI is known for creating better, faster, and easier patient positioning tables for physicians, technicians, and medical directors across the country. "We design our patented specialty beds and tables to improve diagnostic imaging in cardiology, radiology, mammography, and interventional procedures. Our brand thinks about positioning in a 360 degree way—from the patient to the technician to the physician to the hospital. Here's how: Our tables and beds position the patient for the utmost comfort. They ergonomically position the technician to minimize repetitive stress injuries that can be career-ending. They position patients to capture a clearer image for physicians to improve the diagnosis. And, they position the hospital department for increased revenue by increasing patient throughput without sacrificing image quality. Paying attention to positioning is at the forefront of all we do."

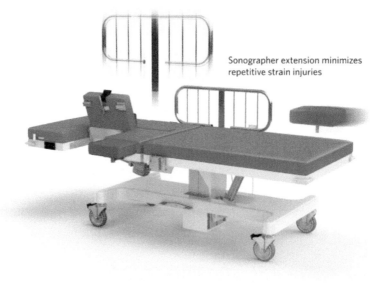

Sonographer extension minimizes repetitive strain injuries

Brady continues, "Perhaps the most important part of our positioning strategy is that we start by positioning ourselves alongside our customers. This is how the company was founded over two decades ago. When we brought our EchoBed to the market it was a co-creation between us and our customers. We believe that direct communication with our customers

position

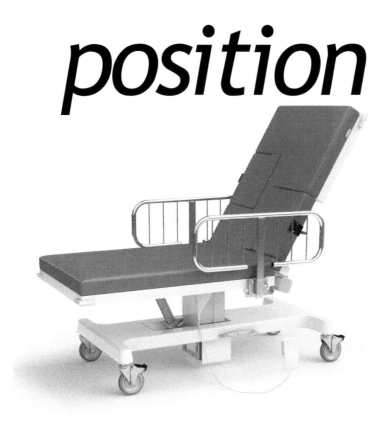

is critical. Our product developers work hand-in-hand with the people who are going to use our imaging tables every day. We work closely with the practitioners, physicians, and technicians to create innovative new products that deliver exceptional results for both patients and staff. We want to understand their concerns and match them with a product that meets their needs."

ThinkAbout: POSITION

How closely are you positioning yourself alongside your customer? As a product developer, do you think about your product's positioning in a 360 degree manner? Do your competitors? Do you focus on just one facet of your positioning when there are more areas that can be leveraged?

ince 1919, way before emailing and texting and tweeting, American Stationery has been celebrating the joy of letter writing. American Stationery launched back when the quality of the paper you wrote on was associated with your own personal reputation. When things like beautiful handwriting mattered. And fine paper texture mattered and professional embossing, debossing, and engraving mattered.

For some people, these things still do matter. And despite the speed of a tweet or a text or the efficiency of a mass email, these folks know that taking the time to write an encouraging word, or send a timely thank you or compose a professional business follow-up on beautifully crafted stationery still matters. These are American Stationery's customers.

Kathy Calderbank, Vice President, Marketing knows that her customers still love having a collection of fine papers in their desk drawers so they can express themselves the old fashioned way. "Our customers want a selection of papers to match to their writing occasions and to express their emotions and personalities. We have created hundreds of options for them to choose from—from classic correspondence cards to colorful notes to vibrant patterns. On any given day, they might write to three different people on three totally different papers. They come to us for a variety of expressions."

The brand leaders at American Stationery realize they are competing with Twitter and Skype and numerous other ways to connect with family and friends. Calderbank shares, "We want to make it easy and convenient for them to dash off a note. That's why we designed one set in particular, our Deliciously Colorful Gift Set. It provides all sorts of options in one container that can sit on a desktop and make dashing off a note simple and quick. In that way, it's an *express* expression! It's also a great gift."

Here's what our customers have said:

"I love the colors as they add so much personality. Highly recommend it!"

"I absolutely love it. Fun, pretty stationery—thrilled that I ordered these as an alternate to some of my more formal pieces."

express

ThinkAbout: EXPRESS

How do your products express your brand values?
Your customers' values? Have you allowed for multiple forms
of expression with your products?

*l*ifetree Café is not your typical organic café or coffee bar. It was created by experts in the ministry resource business, Thom and Joani Schultz, who serve as President and Chief Creative Officer of Group Publishing. Lifetree Café is a place to converse about topics that aren't often discussed in church. Billed as an "hour of stories and conversations to feed your soul," Lifetree Café is like a cozy, weekly, coffeehouse experience where people from all walks of life gather to discuss meaningful issues (ranging from trauma to terrorism to grace to marriage to anger). Lifetree Café serves up provocative topics, a civil and welcoming atmosphere, and a time and space to contemplate important, but often neglected, matters that tug at people's hearts. "We just kept hearing over and over again that churches were struggling to connect with people in their communities. We wanted to help so we created Lifetree Café."

Craig Cable, Lifetree Café National Director, shares this story about how Lifetree Cafe helped a recent participant:

"The topic that brought Ron into our Lifetree Café for the first time focused on the issue of dealing with guilt. The story we discussed centered around two friends who had a falling out years earlier and some lingering guilt as a result of their friendship ending. Near the end of the program during one of the large group discussion times, Ron raised his hand and asked the facilitator a question, "But what do you do with big guilt?" Ron then proceeded to share his story.

"Several years earlier, Ron and his wife were preparing to leave the house to go to their fitness club. The weather that evening was pleasant so Ron suggested going on a walk together instead. His wife reluctantly agreed and together they headed out on their evening stroll. A short time later, they were standing on the curb at busy intersection waiting for the light to turn when his wife mistakenly stepped out into traffic and was instantly killed by a passing motorist. Ron felt responsible for her death because the walk was his idea. But the tragedy didn't end there. Ron was so grief-stricken from his wife's death that he didn't see the emotional warning signs in his son who was also grieving the loss of his mother. Three months later Ron's son took his own life. Ron perceived that his wife's death and his son's suicide were all his fault. And he came to

help

What's brewing at Lifetree Café this week?

Join Us!

"Doing Life. Doing Good."

Lifetree Café that night to find answers and help on how to deal with big guilt.

"Well, the story didn't end there for Ron. He has continued to come to our Lifetree Café and is now flourishing. He's plugged into a local church and several grief support groups. Ron is now helping others who have experienced loss and is showing the same acceptance, love, support, and encouragement that he found at Lifetree Café on his very first visit. Lifetree Café helped him in a way that no other place or person did. This is what we're all about."

ThinkAbout: HELP

Does your product truly help your customers? How can you experiment with ways that it can help in even more meaningful ways? Is there an unconventional approach in your industry just waiting to be tried? What are you waiting for?

hen you put your own name on a brand, authenticity matters. John Thos. Baker IV should know. As Founder and CEO of Thos. Baker, a premium outdoor furniture company, Baker cares deeply about veracity. He is upfront about competitive comparisons (showcasing several on his website), quality workmanship and—most important—exceeding his customers' expectations.

"We think our customers are looking for compelling design and demonstrable value," says Baker. "Our product lines resonate with experienced shoppers who appreciate unique, high quality furnishings backed by a company with a proven history of exceptional customer service and support."

Frances Atherton, Director of Merchandising at Thos. Baker, explains how authenticity is part of every product decision-making process. "How our products are crafted is of great importance to us here at Thos. Baker. Our customers come to us for premium living products with a distinctly American style. They count on us for quality, low maintenance, and durability."

Atherton continues, "Take a look at our Palms dining tables. This exclusive collection is constructed of 304-grade stainless steel and high-tech recycled materials. They feature a contemporary design reminiscent of the famed, mid-century modern Nelson bench that our customers really love."

In today's disposable society, authenticity matters more and more. People want the real deal.

authenticate

ThinkAbout: AUTHENTICATE

If your company's brand name were not already on it, would you put your name on the product you are developing? What adds authenticity to your product? What makes it less authentic? What authenticity variables do your customers care the most about? How are you reassuring your customers that they are getting the "real deal"?

*J*eff Breeden, CEO at Cook's Direct, a leader in heavy duty restaurant equipment and kitchen supplies, believes not only in the power of listening to his customers but in taking their conversations seriously. Listening and responding. Providing expertise and solutions. Looking for opportunities to stretch.

One of the many industrial segments that Cook's Direct serves is the corrections industry. Breeden was in conversation with one of these customers and heard his laments about how the existing plastic cafeteria trays used in feeding the inmates had all sorts of problems. "For one," Breeden explained, "they didn't last. They would crack and stain and were expensive to replace. Food would stick to the plastic and make washing difficult. But the biggest problem he shared was that the intimates would break these trays and use them as a weapon against the officers. Security issues became a huge concern."

Breeden had an idea. Remember when the silicone baking sheets and pans were all the rage? Breeden wondered if this material would be just the secret ingredient for making a great, flexible, non-breakable tray. "While I thought it was a brilliant idea, my vendors and customer just laughed at me. This did not deter me however. I worked with a silicone supplier and we configured the structure of the tray, the durability, the texture of it to allow easy food release and the washability factors. We were certain we solved all the problems. I got the first prototype in and went off excitedly to see my customer. He took it, held it in his hand and proceeded to rip it half. I was mortified. But, I was still not deterred!

"I went back to my supplier again and we worked on engineering round two—really just simple fixes to strengthen the material and trim up the product mold. I'm happy to say that was seven years ago and many,

many sales ago. Our stretchy Cook's Flex Tray is a winner on many functional levels —it doesn't break or shatter. It allows the inmates to hold it in only one hand without folding over and spilling the contents while freeing up the other hand for their beverage.

It washes up easily. But most important, it is 100 percent safe. We solved our customer's #1 security problem. And, it's even less expensive than

stretch

the plastic trays. We stretched our thinking. We stretched our suppliers. We stretched conventional wisdom. All from listening intently to our customers' pain points and believing that we had the expertise to solve his problem."

ThinkAbout: STRETCH

Where might you need to stretch your thinking? Are you listening closely enough to your customers' complaints? Are you challenging your vendors/suppliers/team members to stretch their thinking about costs, components, and other critical factors that make up your product experience?

*b*een there. Done that. Cross it off the bucket list. Inspire someone else to cross it off their list too.

Tony Wheeler, founder of Lonely Planet, the adventure guide-book company he and his wife started in 1974 after their backpacking honeymoon, says that's pretty much how it all began. In an interview with travel blogger Nomadic Matt, Wheeler said, "That's how Lonely Planet started, with people asking us for our recommendations for destinations because we'd been there and done it." Wheeler goes on to tell more of the company's humble beginnings on the website: "We wrote *Across Asia on the Cheap*, sold 1,500 copies and then moved onto our next destination: *South-East Asia on a Shoestring* . . . which led to books on Nepal, Australia, Africa and India . . . which led to . . . present day where the Lonely Planet imprint accounts for some 120 million books in eleven different languages." Not bad for a business that happily and adventurously crosses things off their lists so their customers can too.

In addition to crossing out of the way places off their lists, Lonely Planet also x-es out things that just don't fit their brand or resonate with their type of traveler. The Lonely Planet team spends its travel energy mindfully, x-ing out many options so that their customers can have a journey that is off the beaten path. Their brand is all about adventure travelling, not tourism. Lonely Planet guidebooks don't necessarily have you crossing off the same sights your "been there done that" list as some of their competitors (such as Fodor's, Frommer's). Rather, they want to guide you on the atypical, unexpected adventure. This independent thinking is a big part of the Lonely Planet's point of view. They pride themselves on their editorial independence:

> At Lonely Planet we tell it like it is, without fear or favour. There's a whole world of amazing sights, hotels, travel companies and gear manufacturers out there—and we want to tell you which ones we think are best. But we never compromise our opinions for commercial gain. If you read something written by a Lonely Planet author, you can guarantee they've been there, had a look for themselves and are telling you what they really think. It's trusted advice from a trusted source.

x-ing

For example, Ryan Ver Berkmoes, one of the authors of Lonely Planet's guide *Bali and Lombok* (14th edition), is typical of the Lonely Planet traveler. Although he's been visiting the island for 20 years and has explored almost every corner of the island, "just when he thinks Bali holds no more surprises, he finds, for example, a new seaside temple on nobody's map." And, that's just what the Lonely Planet adventure traveler is looking to put on her itinerary!

ThinkAbout: X-ING

What products are on your brand's bucket list? Jim Collins talks about the power of "stop doing" lists. Is there anything you have "been there, done that" and might want to cross off your product development list? By x-ing out things that are not yours to do, but your competitors', might your point of view become clearer?

*n*o doubt, most of us have been impacted by cancer in some way—a friend, a family member, possibly even ourselves. Having walked that rugged road with others, I appreciated seeing the new partnership between Stand Up 2 Cancer and the Cancer Treatment Centers of America built around the verb *question*. Here's how they describe their new public service online and social resource, The QN2A Project:

> With cancer, having questions doesn't make you weaker. It makes you stronger. The more you ask, the more you know and the more you can stand up to cancer. So we created QN2A.org, a powerful new online resource of all the Big Questions that can help both patients and caregivers after a diagnosis.
>
> We've all been there in the physician's office, your mind spinning. Later, you remember all the questions you wish you'd asked. Because the best answers come straight from your healthcare professional, we've created QN2A to empower you to ask the right questions in those crucial conversations, so you get the best answers—Q into A.

> And, while you're at QN2A.org, help us grow the list by sharing the questions that helped you the most. Together we can find the right answers. Without question.

What a powerful bottoms up "product." A product of questions co-created by all the people most in need of the answers. A product that may just change lives based on these questions. A product that will guide healthcare providers into even more crucial conversations, sooner. A product that will educate and comfort. A product that will provoke even more questions.

Question—simply one of the most powerful verbs we can consider in creating new products or programs or services.

question

ThinkAbout: QUESTION

What question keeps your brand up at night? How do questions fit into your product development process? Are they welcomed? Sought after proactively or simply responded to reactively? Do you know what top-of-mind questions your customers have about your product?

" efresh and renew your home," invites the headline on a recent Pottery Barn catalog chockfull of Spring decorating ideas. "New blooms outside inspire a refreshed home inside. Renew your home with cheerful bedding to celebrate the welcome change in season." The merchants and product developers at Pottery Barn truly have become America's interior decorators. Customers refer to their catalogs as "magazines" right up there with traditional home décor titles and lust after the well-choreographed rooms of inspiration. "If only my house could look like that," is a frequent sigh. Pottery Barn makes that

dream a reality with a plethora of product assortments (by room, by style, by color, by theme, by product type) and by complementary design services offered both in person and online.

Cathy, one of Pottery Barn's Sales Associates, greets customers each week and is part of the friendly, helpful, no pressure atmosphere that the brand strives to create. She shares: "Customers come in our store looking for ways to update all areas of their home—bedrooms, living rooms, dining rooms, patios. We offer so many delightful options from furniture to pillows to tableware accents to linens or rugs that provide quick and easy updates to rejuvenate their rooms each season without a major remodel. But, if they want a major remodel, we can do that too! It's hard to resist our seasonal displays. Customers love the way we present new tabletop ideas, our pattern plays, and even the calm order of our organizational products. They want their homes to look like our stores!"

No doubt, Pottery Barn is in the "continual update" business. By offering its customers ever changing and enticing presentations of visual merchandising, complimentary classes, decorating tips, entertaining tricks, in-home appointments, design tools, and inspirational videos each holiday or each season, Pottery Barn sells service as much as product. It guides customers in making appropriate changes to their homes, and encourage them to do it all over again next season!

update

FISH PULL* -40-0343525 $7

PRINTED CERAMIC KNOBS*
Gray or Blue. -40-0342899 $9

FARMHOUSE HARDWARE COLLECTION*
-40-9574328 Rooster Knob $12 Pig Pull $15

INSTANT
update

Some little details have big impact. Old cabinets, vanities and dressers get an easy makeover when you switch out old hardware for new gleaming metal, ornate glass or smooth ceramic.

PITTED HARDWARE COLLECTION*
Bronze (shown) or Vintage Pewter. -40-3104999
Square Knob $9 Round Knob $9 Pull $12

ANDRICK GLASS COLLECTION*
-40-0343582 Knob $12 Pull $15

MEDITERRANEAN HARDWARE COLLECTION*
-40-0380089 Knob $9 Pull $12

CLASSIC HARDWARE COLLECTION*
Satin Nickel, Bronze or Polished Nickel. -40-2361434
Bin Pull (shown). $7 Knob (shown). $7 Hook $29

ELLA HARDWARE COLLECTION*
Antique Bronze (shown) or Vintage Pewter.
-40-9574336 Knob $9 Pull $12 Large Knob $12

Catalog/Internet Only

ThinkAbout: UPDATE

Do your products help your customers refresh or renew some aspect of their lives? Are you able to marry product plus service in a way that encourages customers to make updates easily? What aspect of your product offer might be ready for an update?

"there is more to life than furniture" declares a bold headline in a recent IKEA catalog. Perhaps a somewhat surprising statement from the world's leading home furnishings company. But if you know IKEA, then you know that they position themselves as Life Improvers. The copy on the catalog spread confirms it: "Everyone deserves to have a beautiful home and still have money left over for other things. At IKEA we're inspired by all the magical moments that happen every day. These moments are what keep us going, evolving and constantly thinking about how to make life at home better, more beautiful, simpler and more affordable."

IKEA improves its customers' lives in myriad ways, with products that are developed with little helps (dish towels and wash clothes with pre-sown hangers on them) to a plethora of ideas for figuring out small space organization to products designed to be kid-friendly, doing double and triple duty and encouraging age-appropriate play. IKEA also offers many customer-centric services in addition to its products: home delivery, picking, picking with delivery, assembly, assembly with delivery, and kitchen installation.

As perpetual self-improvers, IKEA launched an entire initiative called The Life Improvement Project. Here's how they describe it:

> The Life Improvement house is a collection of projects from people around the country who are making positive changes in every room of the house. We want you to submit your projects, which will then be added within our house. Submitting is easy! Just pick a room, tell us your story, and share. You can also browse through the house for inspiration if you're looking for ideas, and even mark your favorites. When you submit a project or add one to your favorites, they'll populate a personal life improvement home of your own to share with friends. Because what fun is being inspired if you can't inspire someone else!

The entire global enterprise rallies around the verb improve. Mikael Ohlsson, president and CEO of the IKEA Group, elaborates on this in his yearly summary: "We are many who want to contribute with heart,

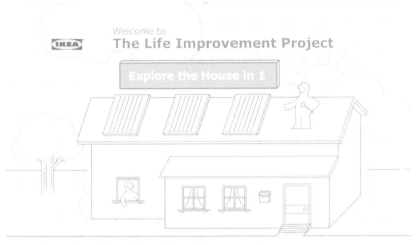

spirit, and all our capabilities to make IKEA a little bit better today than yesterday, and a little bit better tomorrow than today. It is a privilege to be part of this."

Mike Ward, the president of IKEA USA, commented: "Sales results show that people are continuing to find IKEA the leader in life at home; the place to shop for quality home furnishing solutions at great prices. Despite a challenging economic environment, what we offer is relevant to more and more customers. We remain dedicated to growth, a great shopping experience, as well as being a business strongly committed to sustainability."

ThinkAbout: IMPROVE

What is your self-improvement plan to hone your merchandising skills? As a merchant, what are you doing to improve your customers' lives in little/medium/big ways? What improvement project might you launch that would generate customer input into your product development process?

*m*argaret Rudkin, the Connecticut mother who founded Pepperidge Farms in 1937 to help her son's allergies, had a habit of asking her employees, "What's next?" to make sure the business was always moving forward. She herself was a positive thinker and enlightening her customers and advancing optimism is still part of the brand's 76-year heritage.

Pepperidge Farm Goldfish are one of most children's favorite food groups. You'll find those cute yellow (or rainbow colored!) goldfish swimming around most kids' backpacks. It is part of the Goldfish team's DNA to continually challenge themselves with Rudkin's favorite "What's next?" question. They had already created several new versions of their Goldfish cracker products based on closely listening to their customers: Goldfish in bags, boxes, cartons, in multipacks, in grab and go containers, and in 100 calorie pouches. They innovated Flavor Blaster Goldfish and Goldfish Grahams. And, more recently, they jumped into the edible party favor market by introducing customizable packages of Goldfish with your child's photo on them. I am quite certain there are more variations swimming around in the minds of these ingenious product developers.

This time, however, these leaders pushed the traditional product boundaries and created a web  *program* that would further enlighten their brand mission: GoldfishSmiles.

By partnering with people like Karen Reivich, Ph.D., another mother and expert in the field of positive psychology in children, Pepperidge has created a place that causes parents, teachers and children to smile. Full of realistic ideas and activities, the GoldfishSmiles.com site enlightens the brand's mission and its customers' goals by providing downloadable games, conversation starters, and tips as well as relevant information for building and maintaining optimism in children.

enlighten

The Growing Season
Finding Balance
Gardening is hard work, but it's meaningful work we all enjoy together.
Learn More ●

Connecting with my Party of Five
Being Happy
Being mindful to connect with my kids leaves me calmer and more satisfied.
Learn More ●

Balancing It All Through Routine
Finding Balance
To make sure we got together as a family each day, we to created a routine.
Learn More ●

Get to Know Dr. Reivich
Positive Parenting
Our Positive Parenting expert answers questions about being a mom.
Learn More ●

Once in a While She is Wise
Positive Parenting
Things that I see in my kids let me know I've done a good job as their mom.
Learn More ●

Book Club: Dwyane's Pick
Staying Connected
A story about perseverance and how two brothers stood by each other.
Learn More ●

"In today's complex world, teaching young children to increase their optimism and resilience is more important now than ever," Dr. Reivich said when the program launched. Embracing the higher purpose of advancing optimism and creating a service is what the leaders at Pepperidge Farm Goldfish decided to invest in as their "next product."

ThinkAbout: ENLIGHTEN

Try it for yourself—what service could you create to illuminate your brand's higher purpose? How can a brand new service become a product? In what ways could your customers enlighten your product development process?

*t*he mission of The Wounded Warrior Project is simple: to honor and empower warriors. Their vision is profound: To foster the most successful, well-adjusted generation of wounded service members in our nation's history. Their purpose is threefold:

- To raise awareness and enlist the public's aid for the needs of injured service members

- To help injured service members aid and assist each other

- To provide unique, direct programs and services to meet the needs of injured service members

In speaking with Amy Frelly, Warrior Outreach Coordinator, I learned just how life-transforming their work is. "We really are in the honor business. These men and women have given so much for our country and our freedom. Our tagline is: 'The greatest casualty is being forgotten.'

Here at the Wounded Warrior Project, we remember their service, we honor their sacrifice and we witness their recovery process. Many return with injuries such as post-traumatic stress disorder (PTSD) or traumatic brain injuries (TBI) or physical injuries. We honor these men and women through 18 programs that nurture their minds and bodies, encourage economic empowerment and engagement."

The Wounded Warrior Project takes a holistic view of the warriors and their families (including caregivers) in the healing process. The programs address many aspects of their recovery and include: Restore Warriors, Family Support Retreats, Warriors to Work, and Peer Mentoring, just to name a few. Frelly elaborates on one of these programs: "Our Wounded Warriors want and need to develop new career skills. Being unemployed or even underemployed is not where we want our warriors to be. Our Transition Training Academy is a program designed to honor the next career stage in their lives and empower them with the tools and instruction they need to be competitive in the civilian

workforce. It is also through this Academy that corporate America can connect with and hire our newly trained warriors."

There was one more thing Frelly wanted to share about this honoring business: "When you look at our logo, we have one Wounded Warrior carrying another. That is a very powerful symbol for us and represents the brotherhood of this group. Sometimes they are the soldier being carried. Sometimes they are the ones doing the carrying. We firmly believe it's an honor to be both."

ThinkAbout: HONOR

Does your product honor your customers? How can you find additional ways to incorporate extend the practice of respect and appreciation into your product development process?

i first heard about KeepCup from my coffee-drinking Aussie friend, Anita Hendrie, on her visit to the States. Inspired by the founder's daughter's sippy cup, the KeepCup is a barista-sized, aesthetically-pleasing, reusable coffee cup available in fun colors and with the option to be customized or personalized. Abigail Forsyth, CEO of KeepCup, wanted to "create a global brand and to be one of the brands that kickstarted the demise of the disposable."

Hendrie was on an American walkabout and was surprised she wasn't seeing this product in people's hands in our coffee shops. (As this book goes to press, Starbucks has announced that it will be selling a reusable coffee cup.) "The KeepCup is becoming quite popular in Australia," Hendrie said. "It's a product I can't live without. I really hate waste, so I carry my KeepCup in my handbag every day and on all my journeys. I can obviously use it for coffee or tea, but I can also use it for cold drinks instead of using a disposable cup or buying them in a bottle. Sometimes I use it to keep my morning tea in so it doesn't get squashed. And a number of cafes now offer a significant discount ($.50–$1.50) for bringing your own cup, which is always a bonus! They are becoming part of our coffee culture in Brisbane and all over Australia. So many of us really struggle with the easy, throw away culture we live in. My KeepCup is just one small way I can make a difference."

Hearing Hendrie's comments would make Forsyth smile. The stated mission of KeepCup is:

> To encourage the use of reusable cups. We do this by delivering engagingly executed and sustainably procured innovative products. We offer our product in the context of a positive global campaign that strives to make a difference to how people think about convenience culture. We do this by engaging people in three key ways, people who love coffee, people who care about the environment and people who appreciate great design.

Forsyth's kickstart for invention—sustainability—has kickstarted other important product development variables: great designs, colorations, customization, and most important, conversations. In an interview in *Bean-Scene* magazine, Forsyth said, "It's a movement."

kickstart

GO TO THE
KEEPCUP STORE

ThinkAbout: KICKSTART

Do your products connect with a larger purpose? Would your customers say "they can't live without" one of your products? Do they contribute positively to the demise of something else? Are you able to kickstart important customer conversations with your creations?

i'm not sure if any child actually ever really *wants* to get braces, but I know most are grateful for their straight smiles later in life. I know I am. My orthodontic journey started in seventh grade when I had to wear what was called "head gear." Awkward to say the least. The doctor was all business. There were no colored rubber bands. There was nothing fun about it. The best part of the whole two-year endeavor was that I got to miss a few classes a semester for my appointments and then my mom would always take me out for pizza afterwards.

So it was with great interest when I learned that my third-grade nephew and godson, Joseph Martin, was having a fun PRE-experience with a team of orthodontists (Albright & Thiry) in his hometown of Lancaster, Pennsylvania. A few things about his experience stand out. This is what my sister, Nicole Martin shared with me:

"The first thing that I really appreciated as a parent was Drs. Albright & Thiry coming to Joseph's grade school and offering a free screening. Things have changed a lot since we wore braces and it was helpful to learn how early orthodontists want to see the children these days. As part of that screening, we received a coupon for our first visit and a consultation. The second thing that caught my attention was a personal note that Drs. Albright and Thiry sent to Joseph after they saw his photo in the newspaper for winning a Cub Scout activity. He was tickled that they remembered him from the screening (we hadn't even had our consultation yet!). Then, when we went for our first consultation, there was a WELCOME JOSEPH MARTIN! sign near the front of the office. Wow! Did he feel special! I felt that we already had a relationship with these doctors before our first appointment! We've never had an experience like this before anywhere."

Dr. Kristin Albright Thiry told me this is her intent: "We want every patient and parent in our orthodontic office to feel like a part of our family. Our office motto is "changing lives one smile at a time." What this means to us is taking the time to know our patients as individuals, not just their teeth. We have developed office systems, and trained our team members to continually let our patients know we care and welcome them to our office family."

This is all just the beginning. Later Joseph might get to experience

welcome

the Brace Bus which is a free service for middle and high school students where he'd be picked up from school and shuttled to and from his appointments so that his parents don't have to take off additional time from work. And, at the very end, when his braces are taken off for good, he'll get the celebratory goodie bag of all the things he couldn't eat while he was in braces: chewy candy, popcorn, gum.

Getting braces and all that it entails both before and after can be a long journey—in some cases several years—and an expensive investment. Making sure that relationship gets off to a great start is extremely important. Welcoming. Making patients (and their parents) feel cared for in a personal way. Treating their questions with patience and kindness. That's what the practice of Albright & Thiry specializes in.

ThinkAbout: WELCOME

What is your brand's welcome mat experience? Have you spent any time thinking about your customer's pre-product experience? How can you "meet and greet" your customers in advance? In memorable and welcoming ways?

i was already familiar with the radically different publishing company called Twelve and had used them as a model in some of my client work. One of their key points of differentiation is that they purposefully publish no more than twelve books a year. This is a contrarian approach as most of the publishing world simply does not work that way. With over a million books published just last year (according to Bowker's figures), most publishers release a plethora of titles. Most have their A list books/authors, B lists, and C lists and plan promotional dollars and energy accordingly. Out of all those millions of titles each year, only a few will trickle to the top of our country's reading lists and generate worthwhile conversation, information, and entertainment. Most of the rest get lost in the shuffle until they are "remaindered" (like a funeral for a book).

But it was one verb in *The New York Times* description of Twelve that made me linger: "Twelve is an experimental boutique publisher dedicated to releasing far fewer books than a traditional publisher, with the implicit promise that an unusual degree of editing, publicity, and marketing would be lavished on each book." *Lavish.* That really was their brand differentiator. The product developers (in this case publishers/ editors and publicists) were lavishers.

Their mission statement declares: "Talented authors deserve attention not only from publishers, but from readers as well. To sell the book is only the beginning of our mission. To build avid audiences of readers who are enriched by these works–that is our ultimate purpose." They go on to share 12 Things To Remember about Twelve . . . here are just a half dozen:

1. Each book will enliven the national conversation.

2. Each book will be carefully edited, designed, and produced.

3. Each book will have a month-long launch in which it is the imprint's sole focus.

4. Each book will have the potential to sell at least 50,000 copies in its lifetime.

5. Each book will be promoted well into its paperback life.

6. Each book will matter.

lavish

Mission Statement

Twelve was established in August 2005 with the objective of publishing no more than twelve books each year. We strive to publish the singular book, by authors who have a unique perspective and compelling authority. Works that explain our culture; that illuminate, inspire, provoke, and entertain.

Read More

"Even things in a book-case change if they are alive; we find ourselves wanting to meet them again; we find them altered."

—Virginia Woolf

For Twelve, lavishing works. Their books garner rave reviews, bestseller list success, and have won almost every publishing award available. Here's one "product" example that showcases their successful formula: A collection of essays entitled *Argubly* by Christopher Hitchens, which was voted one of top ten books of the year.

Lavishing matters.

ThinkAbout: LAVISH

If you had to narrow your lavishing to only 12 products in your assortment, what 12 would they be? Why? What types of lavish treatment could you bring to bear on furthering their success?

Do you, as a product developer, need to spend more time giving deep attention in order to increase a product's impact?

"*I*t's really Greekin' good," is how Ben & Jerry's advertises its new Greek Frozen Yogurt. Irreverent, quirky, clever, and all about the euphoria of the experience. A zigzag from the other frozen yogurt makers who stress the healthy benefits of frozen yogurt over ice cream. Here's how the company describes it:

> We've combined the creamy richness of Greek Yogurt with our notorious colossal chunks and swirls to bring you Ben & Jerry's Greek Frozen Yogurt. Loaded with all the flavor boldness you'd expect, this creative concoction will release your inner Greek. It our most epic frozen yogurt yet! So get your Greek on and give it a try. We think it'll rock your acropolis. Enjoy!

Ben & Jerry's has taken the ice cream road less travelled since its inception. Zigzagging from its competitors, Ben & Jerry's added focus on progressive social values has always been a big part of the company mission.

According to an article in *Supermarket News*, "Ben & Jerry's jumped into the Greek frozen yogurt market in 2012. Unlike other manufacturers, the South Burlington, Vermont–based company didn't set out to make a super low-calorie product. In an interview with Jody Eley, brand manager for Ben & Jerry's, she shared that 'Ben & Jerry's frozen Greek yogurt ranges from 180 calories to just over 210 calories for a half-cup portion. Our products are not meant for consumers on diets. Our frozen Greek yogurt is lighter compared to our ice cream. The yogurts also contain less fat and more protein than ice cream,' she said."

The new frozen yogurts share the same pint size containers of its ice cream fame, on-trend names, celebrity connections (Liz Lemon) and packaging that have become Ben & Jerry's hallmark. Ellen Kresky, Creative Manager shared this with me: "Zigging and zagging aren't just key verbs for us at Ben & Jerry's. It's the way we do business. Our litmus test for product development, packaging and messaging is: 'Would our competitors do this?' If they would, then we don't!" This is how we've developed our unique personality and point of view. We zig. We zag. We're quirky. We're Ben & Jerry's!"

zigzag

This is a brand that has raving fan support for all its zigzag strategies!

ThinkAbout: ZIGZAG

Have any of your products ever taken a road less traveled?
Has it made a difference? How have your customers responded?
Do you know where your competitors are heading in their
product development efforts? Are you following them or
zigzagging your own path? How might indulgence play a role
in your product development efforts?

P.S: Frolic!

As this book was finalizing development, my husband and I had a business trip to San Francisco. We seized the moment to combine wine with work and we spent a few days blissfully playing in California's wine country. On this jaunt, Dean asked me which company showcased his favorite verb. After 23 years together, I knew he could only mean **Frolic.**

"There is no **Frolic** in *ThinkAbout*," I said.

"Tragic," Dean said. "Stop the presses. You can't *not* have frolic. Frolic is a very important verb in a playful book of inspiration for merchants and brand builders."

I gave that a thinkabout and said the three words he always wishes he heard more often, "You are right."

Frolic, the verb, was right under my nose. I almost missed it. And, it almost didn't happen.

Dean and I have enjoyed seeing wineries up close in all sorts of settings and in many parts of the world, from California to Italy to Australia. Wine is often part of our vacation life. We enjoy visiting the smaller vineyards, definitely off the beaten path, usually family run in some way. We have stayed at wineries for lodging, have had amazingly romantic dinners at the vineyards' edges and have had spontaneous picnics among the roses, olives, and grape leaves midday.

As the playologist in our family, Dean is the one who plans our adventure travel and outings. He had seen the scoop on the Francis Ford Coppola Winery and thought for sure we would *not* be interested. Too big, too accessible, too celebrity and just what is a family pool doing at a winery? So we went everywhere else first on our wine tour but then my curiosity got the best of me. I just had to see what the director of

The Godfather was doing with a winery! We showed up at 3 p.m. It was 90 degrees outside in April. Spring had sprung. Everyone was frolicking!

All the day passes for the pool had been sold (and, we discovered, are sold out for months in advance.) We sat down by the pool bar and ordered some delicious Italian appetizers and a flight of wine and just watched and watched. Francis Ford Coppola was on to something. His winery was totally different from any other we had ever experienced. Moms and dads rented "cabines" for the day so they could shower, change into swimsuits, and store their personal belongings. With the cabine reservation came lounge chairs, towels and a flight of wine. Parents relaxed while their children played in the pool or at the bocce courts near the pool.

We also saw couples sharing cabines and having a glorious day in the sun while being served adult beverages (not just wine—luxury lemonade, cocktails, and daiquiris). Young college girls were celebrating the end of their semester and others were having a birthday rendezvous. This was all happening within the magnificent view of the grapes. Everyone was frolicking!

Francis Ford Coppola explains his strategy:

> I've often felt that modern life tends to separate all the ages too much. In the old days, the children lived with the parents and the grandparents, and the family unit each gave one another something very valuable. So when we began to develop the idea for this winery, we thought it should be like a resort, basically a wine wonderland, a park of pleasure where people of all ages can enjoy the best things in life—food, wine, music, dancing, games, swimming and performances of all types. A place to celebrate the love of life.

Frolic was indeed his guiding verb but many other verbs were also at play. Coppola **directed** his wine scene to be totally different from all the others—no pretentiousness, no excluding children, not even just wine only! Coppola **differentiated** his experience by **zigzagging** when the rest of the industry continues to follow the same, serious direction, fighting for distinction among the grapes. He **transported** people into a wine wonderland. He **juxtaposed** theatre and entertainment with a splash of outdoor frivolity. He **connected** families and friends and **beguiled** them to **linger** all day long. He **glorified** the lost art of kicking back and just being. Coppola believes that "winemaking and filmmaking are two great art forms." We loved how he **integrated** and **promoted** both seamlessly.

After our poolside outing, we went indoors to see his movie gallery (and yes, I saw the infamous desk from *The Godfather*!), taste more wine (and get educated about his Reserve blend and Director's Cut), and then even decided to stay for dinner at his Rustic restaurant on the vineyard, a *tavola* of his *amici* (friends)! We made an afternoon and

Discover our Wines

DIRECTOR'S CUT

"Winemaking and filmmaking are two great art forms."

– Francis Ford Coppola

Cabernet Sauvignon   Cinema   Chardonnay   Pinot Noir

evening out of frolicking at his wine wonderland. I highly recommend it.

Flying back home to Colorado, I thought about the significance of that experience and how it summed up so much of what I wanted to accomplish in this book. No doubt, there are many in the wine industry who frown upon Coppola's frolic strategies. I can only imagine the eye rolling and dismissive conversations that occur behind closed doors. But that is always how it is for innovators. Coppola takes his wine business as seriously as he does his filmmaking. He just chooses to *thinkabout* it differently. The Francis Ford Coppola Winery embraces an iconoclastic spirit and uses a plethora of verbs to create its own playful brand. It is supported by many creative products that all enhance its mission of frolic. For locals and visitors alike, this winery is indeed a Lovemark.

In *ThinkAbout,* I want you to do just that. Play with the verbs. Try these 77 and others on for size. Follow your curiosity. Involve others. Dare to stretch your thinking. Let it lead you to produce something worthy of Lovemark making!

And then, please don't forget one last verb . . .

Pour yourself a lovely glass of wine and offer a **toast** to the reason you undertake all these *ThinkAbout* efforts and create strong brands and purposeful products in the first place—your customers!

Index

ANDREA SYVERSON

Andrea Syverson is the founder and president of IER Partners, which has guided and strengthened brands of all sizes with savvy best practices for creating customers for life. Combining her passion of adventurous listening and working across diverse industries, her "outsider-insider" creative branding and merchandising expertise and objectivity has been valued by companies as diverse as Spanx, Ben & Jerry's, Celestial Seasonings, CHEFS and Boston Proper. She holds an MBA and has dedicated more than 20 years to providing clients, both domestic and international, with innovative approaches to branding, product development and creative messaging. She is the author of two books in which she shares her hands-on approach for both brand building and creating customer-centric products that enhance brands: *ThinkAbout: 77 Creative Prompts for Your Merchandising Muse*, and *BrandAbout: A Seriously Playful Approach for Passionate Brand-Builders and Merchants*. You may reach her at asyverson@ierpartners.com.